MW00936315

An Expat's Guide to Ireland:

Life in a Second World Country

By

Milo Denison

Copyright Information

First Published 2014

Copyright 2014 © Milo Denison

Cover Photography: Adrian Heffernan Photography

Every effort has been made to provide accurate information. However, the author is not liable or responsible for the accuracy of contents provided.

All rights reserved. No part of this publication may be reproduced without prior written permission of the author.

"For readability you need not only basic ideas and solid facts, but also a good collection of seemingly useless information"

- Rudolf Flesch

Introduction

As I stepped off the plane after a nine-hour flight, drowsy eyed and forcing myself to stay awake, I looked for the person that was sent to pick me up. A grey haired fellow in his late 50's/early 60's was standing after the baggage claim exit and holding a sign with my last name and another guy's name on it. He introduced himself, and I received my first taste of a local Irish accent as he loaded us into the car to take us to our respective destinations. The other guy I had never met before was dropped off at a hotel in the city, while I was driven south of the city where my temporary housing, that I would spend the next two months in, was located. I had two months to find a more permanent home in my new city, a city I had never visited before in my life, a city in a foreign country away from my family and friends. I had come in hopes of making new friends and seeing a bit more of the world beyond the lovely state of Washington where I was born and raised. I had arrived in Dublin, Ireland.

This book is written under the assumption that you are moving to Ireland because you are working for a company that is moving you to the country, you are studying in Ireland, or you are possibly moving due to marriage with an Irish citizen. I won't be providing much advice on how to find employment in the country, nor will this book be a standard travel guidebook. There are plenty of those guidebooks available and no need for me to add one more to the list. Suffice it to say, if you're looking to move to Ireland, my recommendation is first try finding a job in the US that will move you over. Most large companies that also have offices in Ireland are experienced at obtaining work permits and other legally required documents to live and work within the country.

As a US citizen, it is difficult to find employment in Ireland without a company's sponsorship. This problem has only increased in the last few years with the downturn in the Irish economy and the increased unemployment rate. For European Union country citizens as a member of the EU, it is much easier to find employment. EU members are not required to obtain work visas, as US citizens or people from other non-EU countries are.

This book is written and researched by an American who moved to Dublin in the summer of 2013 and has lived on the Emerald Isle ever since. A little guidebook, a little relocation advice, and an occasional personal story for entertainment.

Note: Any people mentioned in stories by name have had the names changed. Anyone referenced I'm sure will recognize who they are and will hopefully enjoy my re-rendering of the situation.

My First Day

The flight to Ireland is a long and exhausting one when flying out of Seattle, but it was still early in the day when I arrived, and one bit of advice for travelers to deal with jet lag is to stay awake when arriving and go to bed at the local time to force your body to adjust.

The first order of business then was to call a coworker and friend who had been in town for a couple of weeks and still had one week to go before being sent back to the US. And so, hoping the rates wouldn't be too bad, I called. After a few missed calls and texts, we managed to arrange for him to swing by my temporary housing, which was right off a Luas stop, the local light rail system.

"Let's just head up to Grafton Street," he tells me as we walk to the stop, and he explains how to purchase tickets.

"Okay, cool. I'll need to hit a cash machine as well since I don't have any euros."

Jeremy probably has a few years on me and a lot less hair. He is one of those easygoing types who anyone feels comfortable talking to. Plus he's been on our team in the US for quite a few years, so it makes sense that he would have been sent over for a few weeks to help with an abundance of workload that has been added to the team in Dublin. He is a bit taller than I with glasses on his narrow face. It is nice to see someone I already know on my first day in the city.

As we sit on the Luas train, he explains how to get to the office, which isn't in the city like most of our competitors but near where I am staying instead. I am guessing this is why they put me in a temporary apartment there, with nothing else nearby. I was hoping to be closer to the city center, closer to the location we were heading.

At the end of the line, we got off the Luas next to a large park called St. Stephens Green. Near that we began to walk north on a very crowded section of road designated as foot traffic only. The brick road under our feet was lined with old buildings full of businesses selling clothing, souvenirs, food, and, of course, a few bank cash machines that I could use to get some local currency.

"If I remember right," Jeremy tells me, "there is a pub up here on the right we can eat at and get a beer."

We walk a bit and find a place called The Porterhouse. Upon walking in, I visit my first Irish pub, the first of many Irish pubs I will visit during my time in Dublin.

Coming from the Pacific Northwest where micro-brews are found in every bar and restaurant, I was pleasantly surprised that they had a few brews of their own to offer. We each ordered a pint of beer and food, which included Irish stew for me.

"Cheers," we toasted as the beers arrived, and I tasted the nice cold froth of a much-needed beer after a long flight. My eyes were feeling pretty heavy already, but the excitement of a new place, new sites, and new people, was doing a good job of keeping me awake.

"So, man, what do you think? Think you are going to like it here?" Jeremy asked me.

"I think so, or I hope so anyway. I'm committed to a year for sure, or else I'll have to pay back the relocation money they spent on me."

"I'm envious; I should do something like this. I could really use a change as well."

"Well, I'm sure we will be hiring more. Something to think about."

The food arrived, and the stew was good. Nothing spectacular, this was a pub after all. And it appears pub grub isn't much different in Ireland than it is in Seattle.

"What do you want to do now?" Jeremy asked.

It was early afternoon, and I had quite a few hours to force myself to keep staying awake.

"I don't know; anything you still want to see that you haven't since you've been here?"

After some discussion, we decided on Kilmainham Gaol, an old prison that is now a museum.

We walk over to the red line, which is the Luas that runs east and west through the city. The green line that we were on before only runs north and south. After a short ride, we were at the stop that we thought we needed, and after a bit of walking, a bit of getting lost, and a bit of getting directions from a local, we found the prison—a large dark brick building, a building that very clearly used to house criminals and those accused of being criminals.

My fogged brain was losing its battle to process information as we purchased our tickets and waited for the tour to begin. I had been up for about two days by this point with no sleep on the plane, and had just drank two beers and eaten a stew. It was as if the world was beginning to move in slow motion around me, or maybe I was moving in slow motion, and everything else was following along.

The tour guide introduced herself, took us through some stairs, and began to tell us the history of the prison. She walked us into a room with rows of seating and told us to take a seat for a short video on the prison. The lights dimmed, and the documentary style video started on the large screen in front of us. It was only seconds before my head felt heavy and my eyes began to close, open quickly at the realization, then close again as I fought drifting off to sleep. Luckily, the video was short, and we went from there to the main courtyard and other parts of the prison. I thought to myself, *it would be great to see this at a time when I was awake enough to appreciate it and had a camera with me to take some pictures.*

"Man, I am exhausted." I told Jeremy as we continued the tour.

Jeremy, however, was not tired, and it seemed he had been feeling a little antsy after having been in the country for a week already, not knowing anyone or having anyone to hang out with. We were at opposite ends of the spectrum after leaving the prison and heading back into the city center.

"How about a coffee?" he suggested in an attempt to keep me awake. Agreeing that I was needing something to help give me a kick, we stopped into a coffee shop for a latte. Unfortunately, that wasn't enough, and I had to get some sleep.

"I'm sorry, man. I've got to get some sleep. I'm dying." It was getting late into the afternoon at this point, so I was using that as my justification for heading home early.

"No worries. I understand."

"Cool. So I'll see you when I get to the office tomorrow, then maybe we can make plans for later this week or something."

"Sounds good," he responded as we parted ways, and I went back to my apartment to crash for a few hours.

The few hours of sleeping back in the apartment managed to go until about three in the morning when I woke up and had to keep forcing myself back to sleep. My body was on Pacific Time; I knew that I had to be to work by around eight, and I didn't want to sleep my way through my first workday in Dublin. I eventually gave up on sleep and browsed through the local morning TV channels until leaving for the office.

Overview of Ireland

Language

Everyone in Ireland speaks English, and even with a thick Irish accent, it is still easy for an American to get around and understand anyone we encounter. Most announcements and signs will have both the English and Irish language on them. Irish is recognized as the official language, yet you will most likely find that most Irish don't speak it well and only know a few words, especially within Dublin. Getting into the country, especially in western and southwestern Ireland, it is more common to hear proper Irish being spoken. At least that is what I have been told, I've never experienced it when making my own trips into the country. Irish is required learning in public schools in Ireland. Like in the US where we are required to take a couple of years of a foreign language, after many years of not using it, the language is forgotten easily. There is also a television station that broadcasts only in Irish—the Telefis na Gaeilge.

Weather

The weather in Ireland is generally moderate with little snow during the winter months and only a few days of the summer exceeding 70° F. The climate is heavily influenced by the Atlantic Ocean, resulting in a relatively temperate climate. Due to the high latitude of the country, the summers will have extended days of sun, which will not set until after 10:30pm on some mid-summer nights. In the winter months, the sun sets shortly after 4:00pm, leaving many to arrive at work in the mornings and leave at night, never actually seeing the sun throughout the day.

Temperature is measured in Celsius instead of Fahrenheit as people are accustomed in the US:

Fahrenheit to Celsius
$$[°C] = ([°F] - 32) \times \tfrac{5}{9}$$

Celsius to Fahrenheit
$$[°F] = [°C] \times \tfrac{9}{5} + 32$$

If you don't want to pull out your calculator each time you want to calculate the difference, here are a few rules:

- A temperature difference of 1.8° F is the equivalent of a temperature difference 1° C.
- At sea level, water freezes at 32° F or 0° C.
- 100° F is roughly 38° C.
- The generally desired temperature of 72° F is roughly 22° C.

The joke throughout Ireland is if you are unhappy with the weather, just wait 20 minutes because it will change. Due to the speed with which the weather changes in Ireland, it can be difficult to make plans based on the weather. When going outside, especially during the winter months, it is advised to prepare for rain. And since the country is a large island in the North Atlantic, it is common for strong winds to accompany rain during the winter months.

Dublin
The city of Dublin is a melting pot of nationalities with people from all over Europe coming to the city to study or work. The capital city of the Republic of Ireland has a diverse population of almost two million people in the metro area. Proper Irish pubs abound in the city, as well as cultural activities like museums, theatres, restaurants, and music venues.

Since it is illegal to own a firearm for any reason other than farming or gaming purposes, the murder rate in the country is low in comparison to the US. The police (Garda) usually do not carry firearms, and most violence is related to an occasional brawl at one of the numerous pubs throughout the city. Most Irish are very friendly and social, and Ireland is probably one of the best places for initiating a conversation with people you encounter.

Holidays

One of the advantages of working in Europe versus the US is more vacation days. As a general rule, US citizens get two weeks of vacation per year, while Irish are offered four weeks of vacation. On top of the additional vacation days, there are nine public holidays that most companies honor.

The Irish celebrate New Year's Day, Christmas, St. Patrick's (not always on same days as US), Halloween, and St. Stephen's Day. Instead of celebrating and taking Christmas Eve off from work, Ireland celebrates St. Stephen's day usually taking the day after Christmas off instead. In addition, there are multiple bank holidays that will always fall on a Monday.

New Year's Day	January 1
St. Patrick's Day	March 17
Easter Monday	Easter Monday in April
Bank Holiday	1st Monday in May
Bank Holiday	1st Monday in June
Bank Holiday	1st Monday in August

Halloween	October 31 with the bank holiday on the closest Monday.
Christmas Day	December 25
St. Stephen's Day	December 26

Government Structure

The Irish democratically elected government is referred to as Oireachtas, which consists of a president and two houses: the Dáil Éireann which requires at least one member for every 20,000 to 30,000 people in the county, and the other house, known as the Seanad Éireann. Both houses of government are located in Leinster House in the Dublin city center.

More information: www.oireachtas.ie/parliament

Taxes

As a resident, you will be required to pay taxes on any income earned in Ireland, and the tax rates are much higher in Ireland than the US. The method for filing taxes is a little different; it is advised to consult a tax adviser. My first year in country, since I had lived half the year in the US and half in Ireland, I worked with a tax accountant in both countries to make sure my taxes were filed correctly in both places. The second year, I was able to file my US taxes using online tax services such as H&R Block or TurboTax.

Systems of Measurement

- Weight is usually measured in kilograms (kg)
- 1 kg = 2.2 lbs
- Some Irish people will often refer to body weight in the form of stones:
  - 1 stone = 14 lbs. or 6.35 kg
- 1 Feet = 30.5 cm
- 1 inch = 2.54 cm
- 1 mile = 1.61 kilometers

US Embassy

The Embassy is available to assist US citizens when living or visiting Ireland. The Embassy is a foreboding looking place with a large fence surrounding it and security at the entrance, which is why it is best to call ahead or visit the website if you are planning a visit. Be sure to bring your US passport with you. It is also recommended to visit the website for opening hours as the embassy is closed on a combination of US and Irish holidays, as well as Wednesdays.

Although not required, it is recommended when traveling abroad to register with the embassy. If choosing to do so, this can be done via the website, and a trip to the office is not necessary. Registering allows you to record information about your travels abroad should anything happen and there is a need to contact family in an emergency.

Additionally, the embassy is where you would go for passport replacements, overseas voting, and birth of children registration, visas, and some tax services.

Passport
The passport office is open for walk-in services during morning hours each weekday except Wednesday. Please note for passport services, credit card and checks are not accepted; please bring US dollars or euros. See the website for a full list of needed documents when replacing or renewing a passport.

Voting

As a US citizen living overseas, you are still allowed to vote in elections back home via absentee voting. Each state will have different regulations, so it is worth checking with your local state.

An absentee ballot must be requested at least 60 days before the election to be counted.

Visas

The US embassy does process applications for temporary visas to the US including work, student, and tourist visas. Anyone wishing to immigrate or work temporarily to the US must have a valid visa to travel into the country. In regards to specific requirements, please visit the website.

Useful Links

Federal Voting Assistance	www.fvap.gov
US Embassy	www.dublin.usembassy.gov

Citizenship

If you're planning to live in Ireland for an extended period of time, it is possible to apply for citizenship. This can be beneficial for travel when having the option of using an Irish passport. This opens countries up that US citizens are not allowed to visit, such as Cuba. It is also beneficial when moving through the airport as the citizen versus non-citizen line. The citizen line is usually shorter and quicker. Irish citizenship may be claimed through birth, adoption, marriage, or extended residency.

Dual US and Irish Citizenship

If you're planning on dual citizenship, the US only allows for dual citizenship in select situations. It is recommended to contact the American Citizen Services Unit to identify how this will affect your US citizenship.

Children

As of 2005, children born in Ireland who are not born to Irish nationals are not automatically citizens. Children now born in Ireland are only eligible through parental residency times. Children adopted by Irish citizens are eligible for citizenship. A child born to a parent who is an Irish citizen at the time of birth is considered a citizen, regardless of the parent's residency at the time of the birth.

The education system in Ireland is similar to the system in the US with children progressing from primary to secondary education around the same ages. The grading system, however, is different, although easy enough to figure out.

The cost of education is a little less than in the US, and if a child is an Irish citizen, the cost of a college degree is quite a bit less than what would be paid in the US.

Marriage
In the US, it is possible to marry a US citizen and apply for citizenship through the marriage. In Ireland, this is no longer allowed, and now you must apply through naturalization through residency.

Naturalization through Residency
Generally, the rule for naturalization is that you must have been a resident for five years within the country before you can apply for citizenship and must show intent to live within the country for at least eight years. In order to apply, see the Department of Justice for the application forms and current fees.

Useful Links

Revenue Services	www.revenue.ie
Citizens Information	www.basis.com
Irish Government Website Listings	www.irlgov.ie

A Brief History of Ireland

Ireland has a population of over six million people. Just under two million people live in Northern Ireland and 4.5 million in The Republic of Ireland. In Ireland, roughly 60% of the population lives in urban areas, including the over 500 thousand that live within the city of Dublin.

The island of Ireland is broken into two parts. The south and western portion of the island is The Republic of Ireland, an independent country as of 1922 when it won its independence from the United Kingdom. The northern section of the island is Northern Ireland with its capital city of Belfast. Northern Ireland is still a member of the United Kingdom. Northern Ireland has a long history of violence with the IRA fighting for independence from British rule. In the late 90's a cease-fire was negotiated, and the IRA pledged to honor the cease-fire resulting in peace throughout Northern Ireland.

Covered in bogs and trees, and constantly fighting against the extremes of nature, the first settlers in Ireland arrived around 800 BC. These early settlers built small houses for farming and made life livable through hunting, farming, following the local religions, and trading with one another. As the number of inhabitants grew, the fight for its resources began to grow as well, and the country has experienced a lot of battles and war since.

The Celts began to move over sometime around 300 BC and contributed to the Irish language and way of life. It wasn't until around AD 400 that Christianity reached the country, including Ireland's patron Saint Patrick who arrived in Ireland in AD 432 and influenced Ireland's conversion from the pagan gods to the one God of Christianity. The country has remained devout since with the prominent religion being Catholicism.

Eventually, the country was overthrown by the British in the late 12th century, beginning what was known as the "800 years" of English rule prior to independence in the early 20th century. During English rule, the landscape changed dramatically, going from a country covered in thick-forested trees and bogs to the green grass covered landscape we see now.

The Irish are a resilient people who have always known hard times. The great potato famine, the English rule, rebellions, and crazy weather fills Irish history. During the 1990's, the economy boomed in Ireland bringing in the era of the "Celtic Tiger." Buildings went up at a breakneck pace, and housing prices skyrocketed until the economic crash during 2007 and 2008, forcing the country to take a bailout from the EU central bank and throwing the country into a recession. Even now, years later, the remnants of the boom and bust litter the city with skeletons of massive buildings throughout the city that were started and never completed or that have since been abandoned. Also, talk to anyone about the amount they pay in taxes to pay for the bailouts, and it is apparent in the tone that the cost of the boom and bust hasn't been forgotten either.

To learn more, do an internet search or read a book on the topic. This isn't a history book after all.

Movers

Most companies moving its employees overseas will provide an international moving company to assist with the move. If you are not provided with a company, it is useful to decide well in advance what belongings you will be taking with you and what you will be leaving behind. Most internal moving services will schedule an evaluation before the actual move. This involves someone coming to your house to get an idea of the total shipping size and weight of the items to be moved. The actual movers will then be scheduled later to pack and ship the items. Some moving agencies will carefully list each item that is being packed, while others will be more generic. This is generally dependent on the company and individuals doing the work.

If your employer is paying for your move, verify that they are also covering the cost of moving insurance. If not, it is recommended to purchase movers insurance as items can be damaged in the move process. Items have also been known to disappear when working through customs. So if any high value items are being shipped, be sure to have them listed out on the movers insurance, along with keeping copies of the receipts.

With modern cameras and phones, my recommendation would be to take pictures of items before they are packed. This way, you will have a photographic record of the item.

Mail Services

Today, we can have most, if not all, bills and mail services sent via email versus receiving paper documents. When moving overseas, this is great to allow for payment to credit cards or any other products still being billed in the US. However, as a US resident, there still might be situations where paper mail will need to be received. If you're moving overseas temporarily, it might be useful to look at options on how to receive that mail.

In the US, there are providers that for a fee, you can have your US mail sent to them, and they will scan and email or forward along select mail to your Irish residence. I did a little research in regards to these services for this book, but in the end chose not to use one and had my mail sent to a friend's to hold onto for me.

Irish Postal Services
In the US, we generally only use the post office for one purpose, but in Ireland the postal service is used for a larger array of services. Besides the usual mailing of products and purchasing stamps, you can do some banking at a post office. This is generally used for exchanging currency. The advantage to doing this at the post office is that they offer better rates. You can also get a TV license and pet license at the Irish Post Office. If you have a top-up phone service, you can purchase top-up cards for your mobile phone.

Post offices are open during standard business hours Monday through Friday and limited hours on Saturday. They are closed on Sunday and bank holidays.

If mailing products `Irish Whisky Tour`, be aware that if the customs label shows a value of higher than $50.00, customs duty will most likely be required unless the item is a gift. In this case, you can mail up to a value of $200.00. This works both ways. So if someone is mailing you a product from the US to Ireland, Irish customs may charge a duty when you pick up the package or the package is delivered to your address. Please confirm with the post office before mailing or picking up a package to receive up-to-date information on potential customs fees.

Useful Links

Earth Class Mail	www.earthclassmail.com
Mailbox Forwarding	www.mailboxforwarding.com
USA 2 E	www.usa2me.com
USA Box	www.usabox.com
Virtual Post Mail	www.virtualpostmail.com
Zumbox	www2.zumbox.com

Pets

Personally, one of the reasons it took me so long to move overseas is the love I had for my dog. She really was my best friend, and the idea of shipping her over didn't appeal to me. Having said that, if I had to move and still had her, I would have tried the find the pet friendliest method of getting her into the country as possible.

Like most things, the Irish government strictly controls the import of pets into the country. This is primarily to insure that any potential diseases are not brought into the country. Approximately three months in advance, apply for permission to bring your pet into the country. There is a misconception that pets will need to be quarantined for six months upon entry. This is not necessarily true, as long as you took care of getting the permit in advance and followed the requirements. You will need to provide vaccination records, and the animal must be microchipped. Check with the Irish Department of Agriculture and Food for current entry requirements and to apply for a permit.

Ireland also requires pets to be licensed, even animals born and raised in the country. These licenses can be obtained at the post office, veterinarian clinic, or online.

Useful Links

On-line Dog Licensing	http://www.southdublin.ie/doglicence
Post Office Locations	http://www.anpost.ie

Customs and Immigration

Customs

All shipments going into Ireland are subject to inspection by both US and Irish customs officials. As a new resident you will not be required to pay a duty on household items being moved. If you are taking a vehicle with you, additional permission must be obtained from the Irish Revenue Commissioners prior to being imported. If entering from a country outside of the EU with more than 10,000 euros in cash, you must provide a declaration form to the customs officer at the airport when entering the country.

It is not recommended to take certain items. The Irish government has very strict rules on firearm ownership. Additional applications will need to be submitted through the Department of Justice and Equality for both the weapon and ammunition. Medications should have a prescription to accompany them, and it is recommended to obtain a new prescription after getting settled.

If in doubt about what is allowed to bring into the country, you can contact the Customs Information Office at the website listed below.

If you are planning on moving back to the United States at some point, it is advisable to register items purchased outside of the US with the US Customs office so as to avoid paying duty on the items. Most furniture items can be imported into the US as duty-free as long as you are not planning to resell them. For information on duty rates and requirements, check the US customs website listed below.

Ireland Entry Requirements
Anyone, who is not an Irish citizen, entering the country for longer than 90 days must register and obtain a certificate of registration. At the time of this writing, the fee for the GNIB Registration Card is 150 euros. When going through customs upon arrival, US visitors are only required to show a valid passport. For anyone moving to Ireland, you will need to show a copy of your work permit and letter of employment or school registration.

Note: When traveling in and out of the country, be sure to keep your GNIB card with you. Airport immigration will want to see it when going through customs.

Immigration Office
The immigration office is a series of lines that involve taking a number from one to another. Try to arrive early, but plan to spend most of the day sitting in the office, as the process can be time consuming. You will need to bring with you your work permit or student registration, residency documentation, passport, and basically every piece of documentation you have involving your move to Ireland.

Spouses
Under the Employment Permits Act, spouses of some non-EEA employees who could normally not work in Ireland are allowed to apply for spousal work permits. The same rules apply for applying for a spousal work permit in that the employer must apply for the permit on behalf of the employee. An advantage to this scheme is that the usual permit application fee is exempt. See the immigration office (link below) for detailed requirements and restrictions.

Don't Forget When Moving:
- Passports
- Scanned copies of passports
- Birth certificates
- Marriage license
- Driver's license
- Work Permit
- Letter from employer validating employment
- School registration letter if attending school
- Medical records that might be needed

Useful Links

Irish Customs Information	www.customs.gov
Irish Naturalization & Immigration Service	www.inis.gov.ie
Irish Revenue Commissioners	www.revenue.ie
Department of Justice and Equality	www.justice.ie
Graebel Quality Movers (this is who I used)	www.grabel.com
US Customs	http://cbp.gov

A Day at Immigration

Just like you can always expect a road construction project to have five guys watching while one guy is working, you can always count on a government office to be understaffed with the slow and unhelpful behind windows and desks. While the waiting room is full of unhappy people sitting and waiting, the wooden benches are lined with people from all nationalities, communicating in numerous languages, and children are running around and crawling across the dirty wooden floors, some eating whatever food products they brought with them. An overall aura of misery fills the space, as I acknowledge that some things are universal when it comes to the government, no matter what country you are in. And this is what I see before me as I enter the immigration office.

Looking around, there are lines, numbers on the booths, and no clear indication as to which line to go in first. Jill, the lady whom my employer has contracted to take me around and get my documents set up for life in Ireland, knows exactly who I need to talk to at each stop. Unfortunately, she has no control over the speed at which I get through any of the lines. She is probably in her mid-50s or so, tall with short graying hair and a friendly, chatty way about her. She has the perfect personality for someone who spends most of her time taking people around and sitting in government office waiting rooms.

We take a number, 87, from the man hunched behind the Plexiglas window and sit down with the rest of the people who would rather be anywhere but where we are. Looking up at the screen, we can see they are currently on number 35. Jill had picked me up a little before 9:00 in the morning, driving me first to the immigration office, knowing that it could be the longest on our list of stops for the day. After sitting for about fifteen minutes and watching the screen to see it work its way up to our number, it was clear they weren't going to be getting to my number anytime soon. We decided to walk across the street to a coffee shop, feeling it would be a much more pleasant location to waste an additional hour or two of my life. It was the first healthy substance I had eaten in days, after airline food and quick bites while traveling was all I had consumed. I enjoyed a nice healthy smoothie.

"Are you sure you don't want anything else?" she asks, and is offering to buy more in an attempt to get me to eat.

I don't bother to explain how a healthy smoothie after days of travel, jet lag, and the general stomach indigestion that goes along with excessive time zone changes and crappy food is exactly what my stomach needed.

"No, I'm fine. Thanks," I respond. "I generally don't eat much for breakfast."

After sitting and chatting for a bit, we head back to the immigration office and can see they have worked through a couple more numbers. They're nowhere close to my number—87. Following her guide, she suggests we run to the PPS (Personal Public Service Number) office. It's not too far away from the immigration office, and Jill expects we could make it back in time. The PPS office is where I get my public service number, or local equivalent of a social security number. I can't get paid without making sure I give some of my income to the government, after all. They have to pay the fine people working behind the counters that I will spend my day interacting with.

The PPS office is relatively empty except for a few mothers, families, and plenty of children crying or happily screaming. Jill informs me that the local equivalent of the welfare office is located there as well for mothers in need of public assistance.

It is probably a little after 10:00am by this point, as we are sitting waiting for my turn. Jill occasionally tries to engage me in conversation, which I try to participate in as well, but I would rather be sleeping. She tells me stories about her son who recently moved to New York and is working twelve-hour days in the banking business. *Welcome to America*, I think to myself. It's the country with half as much vacation days, and nearly twice as many work hours in a week—a country with the majority of the population also in favor of legalized marijuana. Is there a correlation, perhaps?

It doesn't take long to get through the PPS office. They take my paperwork, take my picture, and send me on my way. Jill and I hop in the car and race back to the immigration office in the hopes we haven't passed my number. "If we have, I can always come back some other time," I tell her. I have three months to get this done and have no interest in taking another number and waiting. She drops me off near the building while she goes to go find parking. I instantly take a wrong turn, walk a block out of the way, hustle back and around to find the building that Jill has beat me inside. We find that they have worked into the low 70's. There's still plenty of time to spare. So, we sit our skinny asses back into the wooden benches and wait. I half drowse while Jill sends text messages, checks e-mail, and updates parking on her phone—a nifty system I think. For street parking in Dublin, it is possible to extend parking via a text message versus having to walk back out to the car each time to extend it. Seattle, pay attention! Being a tech savvy city, you should set this up.

In what seems like forever, they finally get to my number. The guy working seems young and well kept. He's not so friendly though. Each of the booths is behind Plexiglas windows, where people slide documents under for the person on the other side; it's like going through the drive-up window at a bank. I slide him my passport and proof of residence. He asks me some questions that I have him repeat a few times, since I am having difficulty hearing through the slide under the Plexiglas, before I can answer. Then I am told to go back to my seat for the next step in the process. And so, I go back to my seat, sit, and wait for my name to be called again. Another 45 minutes goes by when I hear, "Milo Denison - American," over the speaker system. I'm then taken into a back room where a short, portly, and unhealthy looking woman slowly walks me through having my fingerprints scanned. The machine reminds me of an office printer. It stands as high as three feet tall with a screen on the top. We can see each fingerprint as it is scanned and watch it inform us of the good scans and the bad scans that had to be done again. One nice thing about technology is there's no ink all over my hands to clean off as she concludes my scans and sends me back to the large, dreary room to wait for the next stage of the process.

"This shouldn't take long," Jill tells me as I sat back down, "all they need to do is print your card, and you are done. I think you can guess if this is going to be a quick wait or not.

You wouldn't think they could come up with a more depressing location than the waiting area, but they did manage to do that in the restrooms. The rooms glow with a fluorescent blue light that is reflected off each surface including the long stainless steel urinal. The men must stand shoulder to shoulder and inhale each other's warm urine fumes as we pee next to each other with eyes forward in an attempt to pretend the other's slowly draining urine sack is less than an arm's reach away. The urine also reflects the blue glow of the light, a color that I am told is to prevent a drug user's desire to shoot up in the toilets. Not being a heroin addict, I can't validate the truth of that statement, but I can imagine any attempt at using a narcotic in the piss steam-filled room would result in a bad trip.

I go back to the waiting area, and we continue to wait and wait. After sitting for longer than Jill thought it should take, she goes up to the window staffed with a very unhappy looking man to ask about the delay. The unhappy man looks up with his tired worn eyes, in a way that said he didn't give a shit about the delay, and responds with almost as such in words that we would just have to wait. And so, we wait some more. We wait and watch others get called to pick up ID cards. We wait while I try to remember if anyone being called had been behind or in front of me for the finger printing line. Around 1:30 in the afternoon, feeling very frustrated Jill goes up again. I could hear her saying my name and nationality; I think to myself that they were going to intentionally drop my card to the bottom of the pile in response to her pushing.

"I don't know why it's taking so long," she says as she returns. "It's never taken this long before."

Not long after that, a guy flags us over to one of the windows and says he doesn't know why it's taking so long to get my card either.

"They sometimes get held up when bringing them back here from the other office," he tells us.

Seems kind of odd to me that they just couldn't print the card at the same location, but then again that could be why I don't work for a government agency—there are too many ways to improve efficiency in my head. The man behind the Plexiglas continues to tell us that we will need to come back the next day, just go straight to the window, and they should have my card by then. Personally, I am too tired to care at this point in the day; I just want to get to the next stop, set up a bank account, and then get home to sleep for a few hours. Having only been in the country for a couple of days at this point, I haven't quite switched to the local time zone for sleep. Jill, however, is a little offended as we leave. I think there is a level of Irish pride in her bothered by the example that is being set by her country.

We leave and finish the errands before she drops me off. I attempt to stay up a little longer but end up falling asleep on the small sofa in my temporary housing. The next morning, she picks me up again; we are able to pick up my card right away with no real explanation as to the delay. She then drops me off for my first day in the office at my new job, immigration card in hand. It's a card that has to be renewed once a year, and I look forward to the same passive faces waiting for me next year with the exception that by then that something will happen, someone will make a mistake, and instead of one person to deal with in each line, there will be a second or third to check the work for the first—all of which adds to the series of checks and balances.

Finding an Apartment

When looking for an apartment or house, it is important to remind yourself this is not the United States. America is known for its large cars, houses, and lifestyles. Europe is not, and Ireland is no exception.

In the US, it is customary to bring your own furnishings to an apartment. You will find in Ireland that almost all apartments come furnished. Some will even supply a basic set of dishes. This can make it hard to decide what to take with you from the US. If possible, try to find a place before you have your stuff shipped. If that's not possible, my advice would be if your employer is paying for shipping, take what you think you might need. If you don't end up needing it, you can always sell it later. If you are paying for shipping, leave it and either hope it's included in your rental or buy it once you arrive.

In Dublin, it is an owner's market right now. Most property owners can get away with putting little to no effort in maintaining properties and get high rent, as there are more renters than properties. This will be worse the closer you get to the city center. Many properties tend to be leased through an agency, and unlike the US where they are happy to get an employed stable renter, in Dublin that only gets you in the door. From that point they have to like you.

Leases and rental contracts are similar in Dublin as they are in the US. You will be required to sign a lease agreement, most of which are twelve-month contacts. A deposit, usually equal to a month's rent, will be required at the signing of the lease. Be sure the lease calls out who is responsible for what charges, such as waste collection and electricity. Just like any other lease agreement, be sure to document any damage to the apartment or house, furniture, and any other items to be sure that the deposit will be returned upon move out.

Size Might Matter
The smaller the included appliances and furnishings are, the smaller the house or apartment will usually be as well. This goes along with their compact living lifestyle. If you bring your bedding with you, check the bed size in comparison; most European beds don't match up.

Rental Sites
- www.daft.ie
- www.rent.ie
- www.property.ie

Buying a House
It is difficult to buy a home in Ireland in comparison to the United States, especially if you moved from the US and don't have long financial records in Ireland. With the economic downturn, housing costs have dropped quite a bit, but prices are still high in comparison to the rest of the country with salaries not much higher.

There is no MLS in Ireland, so the same websites used to find an apartment are also used for finding a home to purchase. As with the US, it is customary to go through an agent when buying a home.

Apartment Hunting

As I owned my last two places of residence back in the US, it has been quite a few years since having to go through the ordeal of apartment hunting. And now that I have had to do it again, I would like to go back to owning my own home once again.

Since moving to Dublin, I had been looking online occasionally, wandering the streets exploring, and asking coworkers, but for the most part, I had been taking my time apartment hunting since I was living in company-provided housing for the first few months. The temporary apartment had an extra bedroom to accommodate the friends and family who never came and visited, and even had a private bathroom for them, which never got used. It had a dishwasher and one of the wash and dry combination units that is so oddly popular in Ireland for laundry. The place even had a cleaner who came once a week to clean up the mess I never made. It wasn't perfect though; the massive balcony looked upon a courtyard in the back that always seemed to have loud children playing in it. And the remote control battery cover had been lost and taped over, which would occasionally stick to my hands when I used it.

But, as they say, "All mediocre things must end." After talking to people and doing a little exploring. I narrowed down my preferential areas for living and the appropriate amount of rent I wanted to pay. I knew I wanted it to be as close to the city center as possible for exploring my new city, but not exactly in the city center due to my light sleeping and desire not to listen to traffic and people drunk late at night wandering down the street. I knew from talking to people that the south side of the river was the better choice in regards to class of people, so I limited my search to the even numbered area codes. I also wanted to be within a ten-minute walk of the Luas light rail that I would need to take each day to get to work at the only large software corporation in the city that didn't have its office in the city center. Ranelagh was at the top of my list. Just south of the city center, it was within walking distance and on the Luas line. The buildings were old, and in my opinion, had more character than any modern apartment. Not far from that was Portobello, a little closer to the city and a bit pricier with a nice long canal running through it for leisurely strolls. From those two locations, I expanded out. One of my main reasons in moving to Dublin was to travel, so when looking at apartments, size wasn't an issue. The ones online in my price range all looked small. I'm not a big guy, and hopefully any girl I would be bringing home would be smaller than I. I felt my standards were low enough that finding an apartment should be a snap. After all, I had a good job, I'm a responsible and clean adult, and I didn't know anyone, so it was not like there were going to be massive parties at my place.

I thought about calling as I was looking, but one of the perks that came with the relocation is that is my friend Jill from the Irish relocation services was going to take me around to look at apartments—yes, the same Jill whom I spent a day with hanging out at the immigration office. She contacted me the first week of August, and we discussed locations and my price range. I even sent her a few of the places I found online and wanted to take a look at. She replied a few days later with an itinerary and the list of places. Two were out of my price range, one was out of my range and location, and only one on the list I sent was in my location and price range. She told me that she called the others but didn't receive callbacks. At the time I wondered if she did, but after my own experience, I now believe her.

I replied letting her know that the overpriced out-of-area one wasn't worth looking at and sent her a link to another one I found and would like to look at. She picked me up the Thursday morning we were scheduled to look at the place, and off we went. I had only told my boss that I would be out of the office for half the day. Based on the small list, I knew it shouldn't take long to find a place. The first place was in a great location, only a few minutes' walk to the Luas that I take to work, and was an old brick house converted into apartments. It met my description precisely. The apartment for rent was on the first floor, and as we walked in, the first thing we see is that it is a very large place. It was the whole first floor of the house. The living room has a large fireplace that looked like it hadn't been used in years, and there is a large set of double doors that leads to the bedroom. The bedroom was as large as the living room, if not larger. The lone bed looked out of place in such a large space with its pale blue painted walls and massive windows looking out into a poorly maintained backyard overgrown with grass and weeds. Through a door in the bedroom was the bathroom. There was a small, old claw-foot tub with a shower curtain and a shower head attached to the wall next to it; it was clear that it was installed by someone who didn't want to spend money on the place or didn't know anything about home repair. Back in the living room, there was a wall, of sorts, that had been built to separate the space for the kitchen appliances. I wouldn't call it a kitchen as it was such a small and oddly designed space that one person could barely fit in it. We stood and talked to the guy for a bit, asked him a few questions about the place then thanked him and moved to our next location.

"So, what do you think?" Jill asked as we were back in the car.

"I like the location, but it was cold in there now in the middle of August. I wonder what it would be like in the winter."

She agreed, and was very disappointed in the kitchen as well.

The next place it turned out to have just been rented, which was unfortunate because it was exactly what I was looking for. It was just off a main area in Ranelagh. It was also in an old house that had been converted to apartments, but this one was clean and well maintained. It actually had a kitchen, and the bathroom had a shower that didn't look like only a trapeze artist could get in and out of. It wasn't perfect, however. The downside is that it had communal laundry room, but there were only four units sharing it, and there was no additional charge for the laundry. The reason the lady had agreed to show it to us after renting it was because she said the place across the hall was going to be available, and it had the exact same layout. I told her I was interested, and she said she would get back to us when it became available.

The next one from there was the one that was priced higher than what I wanted to pay, and not in a location where I wanted to live. Walking into the building, I could see through the hall out a back door that led to a play area. We turned left, then right into the apartment he was showing. It was ground floor and had a very odd use of space. It had an entrance area with a door to the living room, a separate door to the bathroom, and another to the bedroom—all closed. The worst part was right outside the bedroom window was the play area. I could only imagine how miserable it would be trying to sleep while children were playing literally outside my bedroom window. The kitchen was fine, and it had a small washer/dryer combo. But it was a crappy layout with a bunch of unnecessary doors and a waste of space. Plus, it was priced at 950.00 a month, about one hundred more than I was interested in paying. I moved to Dublin to see Europe, not so that I could spend money on a small bizarrely laid out, potentially loud apartment in a location where I didn't want to be.

The next one was the same price as the previous, but a nice location with parking. Parking I didn't need, but whatever. The place was on an upper floor and in a quiet area. The apartment was not too poorly laid out, and so far it was the one I liked the most. It felt quiet and had a wisher/dryer. I just needed the current resident to move out and clean up after themselves. After that came a tiny studio with a fold down bed. I am okay with the idea of a studio, but after folding down the bed, I could see that my short ass would have been too tall for it, not to mention that there wasn't any place to sit beside the fold down bed. On the plus side, it was in a quiet area and only a five-minute walk to the Luas.

I was getting tired and had to get back to work; I honestly felt that I would have better luck on my own by this point. Back at the office, I called and emailed a couple places and scheduled two viewings for that Saturday. They were both in the area I wanted and both in my price range. The first was for 12:00 in Ranelagh with the agent, a guy named Sean. I arrived a few minutes before 12 at the address, but there was nothing that looked like the front door to the apartment from the picture. A red door, a brick building, which described most buildings in the area, yet nothing near the address was fitting that description or look. So I called him at the number I had for him and left a message letting him know I was there, or at least in the area, and wanted to confirm I was in the right place. I waited, walked around a bit, and checked out the little store on the street and the restaurants in the area that looked to me to have nice character to them. At about 15 after, I called again and left another message trying to be as nice as possible, all the while I was very annoyed. I didn't call a third time.

The next location was fantastic. Unfortunately, that's all it had going for it. The apartment was on the ground floor, incredibly tiny, and had mold growing on the ceiling of the bathroom. The mold reeked throughout the unit as well. When I looked at the ceiling the owner said, "I'm going to need to do something about that," in a way that implied if he could rent the place without doing something about it, he would. We discussed the place, and I really did think about getting it just based on its location. But I knew a girl once who told me about a place she lived in with a lot of mold. She got mold poisoning. I told him I would call him and let him know if I decided to take it, but still thinking I could do better, I went home to give it some thought and decided not to rent it. I was nice enough to call him and leave him a message letting him know.

I continued the search through the weekend and decided to go for the pricey place with parking. It was quiet and good location. So, I called Jill and left her a message that Sunday. Feeling a little desperate, I looked the rental up online and called the agent we met with directly as well. He also didn't answer, and I left a message. When Jill called me back on Monday, she informed me that it had been rented. I'm still kicking myself for not taking it when I had the chance, letting my confidence and apartment hunting experience in the US get the better of me in Dublin.

Continuing the search, I called more places without receiving any callbacks, or if they did answer the places were usually rented. I went and looked at another one that week and told him I wanted it. The agent for this place said he would let the owners know and would get back to me. He never did, even after I called him multiple times and left messages. If it weren't for the different names, he might as well have been the same agent who didn't call me back from before. Another one I looked at the same night in the same area was huge. I told him I was interested. He was in the process of painting the place and didn't want to rent it until the following week. He said he would call me when he was ready to rent it. I'm sure you can guess by this point if he called me or not.

What I learned from this experience is that most agents and landlords in Dublin are assholes. Sure, most are anywhere, and maybe it has just been so long since I've had to rent a place that I have forgotten what a crappy experience it is. Most everyone I have met in Ireland has been awesome, but I guess jerks are in every country; in Dublin, they are landlords with apartments to rent. But it really has been a miserable experience. I mean, come on, I work for Microsoft. It's not like I'm not going to pay the rent on time. I have a nice upstanding citizen look to me.

Eventually, I went to look at a place one evening with less than two weeks before needing to be out of my temporary housing. The location was great, right near the city on Upper Leeson Street, and only a few minutes' walk to the Luas. The downside was it was the front apartment on the second floor, or first floor if you are Irish, and was on a busy road. The place was recently remodeled, had a nice bathroom, and was in the price range I wanted. There were two other people looking at the apartment at the same time. After the incident with the other places I wanted and taking too long to decide on them, I called the owner right there with the agent in front of me and told him I wanted it. I also gave the person showing it to me a deposit that night to secure the apartment.

The kitchen didn't really exist; it was more of a nook carved into the side of the living room with barely enough room for a mini-fridge, small stove, and small sink. The entire apartment could fit in the living room of my temporary housing. But after my search to that point, I didn't want to risk not taking it.

After spending my first night in the new place with no sleep due to the noise from the road, my worries were confirmed on the noise problem. But, at least I had an apartment, and I could officially call myself a resident of Dublin.

Setting Up Services

Banking

Banks and utility services will require proof of employment and residency when setting up services. You will need to request this from your employer upon arrival to be provided to the bank. They will allow for a temporary notice of residence from wherever you are staying, but after six months, bank regulation will require a utility bill to verify actual residency. If you are married, it is a good idea to have both your names listed; if this is not an option, have one bank account set up in each spouse's name.

When opening an account, take the following with you:
- Passport
- Proof of employment
- Proof of residence (utility bill or letter from owner)
- PPS Number

There are cash machines throughout the city, and even though banks in Ireland charge account maintenance fees that are usually not charged in the US, they do not charge additional withdrawal fees if you are withdrawing cash from another bank's ATM.

PPS

The PPS number is an equivalent of the social security number in the US. This will be used for tax purposes and other social services. You will also need a PPS for banking, as well as to apply for a driver's license. Visit www.welfare.ie to apply after you have moved. To apply, you will need a birth certification, proof of residence, and passport.

Electronics
Electricity costs tend to run a little higher in Ireland than in the US. Also, the electricity in Ireland is 220V instead of the 110V electric system in the US. This is important to note if you're bringing electronic devices with you, as you will also need to purchase a step down transformer so that your high powered devices such as televisions and game systems will work. I would recommend spending money on a high quality step down transformer, as you could end up with a fried television just using a plug adaptor or lower quality transformer. Most smaller devices will work fine with a standard plug adaptor.

Region Locking
DVDs are sold in markets for specific regions. What this means is DVDs purchased in the US will not work in a DVD player purchased in Ireland or the rest of Europe. This also goes for gaming systems such as Xbox and PlayStation. So if you plan on watching your old DVDs, you will need to bring your player with you, and you will need to purchase any new DVDs on trips to the US.

When it comes to your television, note that the US uses NTSC for broadcast signals and DVD encoding. If you do decide to bring your television, you can use it, but it won't receive inputs from local cable and television companies. If you bring your TV, you will also need to bring your US DVD player and gaming systems to work with it.

Recently, some manufacturers have started releasing products without these regional requirements. For example, the Xbox One no longer has region locked games, so an Xbox One purchased in Ireland will play Xbox One games purchased in the US and visa-versa.

Useful Links

Bord Gais - Gas	www.bordgais.ie
ESB Electricity	www.esb.ie
Electric Ireland	www.electricireland.ie
Water	www.oasis.gov.ie
Waste Management	www.dublinwaste.ie

Internet Service Providers
One nice thing about Ireland in comparison to the US is the amount of competition in the service provider markets. The increased competition is a benefit to the consumer, so it is possible to find relatively decent rates.

When setting up internet service at home, most services are bundled so you will be offered cable television and home phone services along with your internet service. Check the place you are moving into to see if it is already wired with a specific provider. Unlike the US where they will often use the same cable input or phone line as the previous provider, in Ireland ISP's will wire separately. This could be an issue if you are renting, so you might have to choose what has previously been installed in the building.

A couple of websites worth checking out to get reviews and ratings on service providers is www.getbroadband.ie and www.ratemyisp.ie.

ISP Links

BT Ireland	www.btireland.ie
digiweb	www.digiweb.ie
Eircom	www.eircom.net
Imagine	www.imaginebusiness.ie
Irish Broadband	www.irishbroadband.ie
Magnet	www.magnet.ie
Sky	www.sky.com
UPC	www.upc.ie
UTV Connect	www.utvconnect.com
Vodafone	www.vodafone.ie

Wireless Phones

Ireland currently has a large selection of wireless phone providers to choose from, and just like ISPs, it is possible to find rates much lower than what is available in the US. The wireless phone providers all use SIM technology on the GSM European network versus the CDMA that many US carriers use. If you are moving from the US and have a phone that accepts SIM cards, the phone should work in Ireland as well if it is unlocked.

It is relatively easy to set up service with a local provider. Most offer similar plans to what we are used to in the US. Also, prepaid and top up plans are very popular throughout Europe. These services are good if you already have a phone or plan to pay full price for the mobile phone. If you are not sure how long you are going to be in Ireland, these offer a low cost alternative to long-term contracts. Most contracts are for 12 months; the Irish public hasn't been so willing to accept the 24-month contracts that many US providers are moving customers to.

In Ireland, all mobile phones use a prefix prior to the number, usually 085, 086, or 087 depending on the carrier. For example, if you have a wireless phone through Meteor, your number would start with a 085.

When dialing locally or within Ireland from your mobile phone, you will need to dial the prefix prior the calling the number. For example, in Dublin you would need to 01 prior to the number. This is only necessary when dialing from a mobile phone. A landline phone will not require this if dialing from Dublin. If you wanted to call Dublin from, say, Galway, you would still need to dial 01 because Galway has a different prefix. This prefix is the area code. You just dial the area code and number to connect. Dialing numbers in Ireland can take a little getting used to for anyone coming from the US where we are accustomed to dialing just the area code and number.

Some Mobile Providers

02	www.02.ie
3G	www.3ireland.ie
Meteor	www.meteor.ie
Vodafone	www.vodafone.ie

Dialing Home

To make international calls from Ireland, you will need to dial 00 before the country code. The country code for Ireland is 353. And when dialing back to the US, the country code is 1. So to call the US, you would need to dial 001 before the local US area code and number.

With modern technology, it is rare that you would be dialing long distance directly from Ireland to the US. Skype is a useful tool for this that will allow you to video chat with anyone back in the US and won't charge you excessive long distance fees. Many cellular companies are also offering international calls with rate plans as well.

Netflix and other Streaming Services

Due to licensing laws, you will find what you get from these streaming services to be different than what you received in the US. Netflix, for example, has a smaller selection when it comes to shows and movies in Ireland.

TV License

Ireland requires that anyone with a television in his or her home pay a TV license. This is required even if you don't have the television set up to receive over-the-air signals. This is an annual fee of 160 euros. This is a common fee in many European countries that anyone coming from the United States will have to get used to. The justification for the fee is that it funds local programming that would not otherwise be possible without it. This is similar to how US taxpayers fund PBS and other public broadcast services. The difference is that this is included with the income tax in the US versus having to pay out-of-pocket each year. You can purchase

your TV license at any post office in Ireland or online at
www.anpost.ie.

The Irish government has inspectors that will actually knock
on your door at random times and request to view your TV
license. Failure to provide proof of the license is up to 1,000
euros for a first offence and 2,000 euros for subsequent
offences.

Two Shipments

"Please explain why you are using your second shipment now, after having been in the country?" the email asked.

What I wanted to respond with and what I actually responded with were totally different. What I wanted to say was, "Because I can, so piss off!" What I typed in response was more along the lines of, "When I moved over, I didn't know where I would be living or what types of furnishings would be in the apartment that I rented. So, with the shipment services that were provided to me, I took a minimum amount of items. Now that I have a more permanent place, have been in the country for a few months, and since the company I work for is covering the cost of a second shipment, I am choosing to use it." This was in response to Irish customs who was questioning why I didn't use my full shipment allotment when first moving to Ireland.

When moving over to Ireland, I had the ability to send a smaller shipment of items by air, and a larger shipment of items by sea. The air shipment being the quicker one, and since I had never been to Ireland before and had no real idea how long I would be in country, what I would need or potentially be moving back, I decided to keep the items I was bringing with me small. This way, if I had to pay to move stuff back myself someday, I could reduce the amount I would need to spend. Besides, the idea of living with less has always appealed to me. And so, when initially moving, I was able to get everything in just the air shipment.

I had fired off a quick email to the relocation contact that was provided for the move and asked if it was possible to use the sea shipment now since I hadn't used it originally. The contact checked and responded that yes, this was an option, that it was good for one year after my initial move. And so, I made plans to kill multiple birds with one stone by booking my Christmas holiday. During that time, I could visit my family and give them the pleasure of my company while taking care of moving some stuff around, including my second shipment to Ireland.

Back in the States, I first stopped at my condo that was being rented out to some friends to check on it and lecture them for not doing a good enough job of taking care of it. I then visited with family for the holiday, then removed stuff from storage to meet up with the shipper who arrived promptly on time (unlike the first air shippers who arrived four hours late) and watched them as they quickly packed my items.

In discussing living in Ireland with the guy in charge, we discussed the countries that he had visited in the past; I informed him how it would have been nice if they let me ship alcohol due to the high cost of alcohol in Ireland. A bottle generally costs almost twice what a person would pay in most US states.

"I'll let you ship some if you want. I just won't write it on the manifest."

"That would have been nice to know before you got here," I responded, actually thinking about making a run to the store to pick up a couple bottles real quick. This was a stark contrast—the first guys who packed my things when first moving over meticulously cataloged each item, and the second set of guys made sure everything was properly wrapped, but didn't seem too concerned about cataloging.

"I've seen Irish customs go through and take stuff, so I've found that if I don't list everything, they are less likely to take anything," he told me. And to be honest, what he said wouldn't surprise me. I didn't go into detail above on the numerous emails I had with them where they would ask for something, I would send it, then they would want something else. But the reality is, the most likely reason they didn't list everything in as much detail as the first guys was the time necessary to do so. I wasn't concerned as most of this second shipment items were things I didn't care much about anyway.

After they packed up and left, I finished my trip and was back to Ireland to wait on my shipment's arrival. As what seems typical of government offices, I had to respond to some emails justifying my shipment and speak on the phone to someone asking me about living in their country with, "Why? Are you worried that I'm illegally trying to move from a country with a lower unemployment rate and higher salaries and where I could legally get a job, to a country with a higher cost of living, higher unemployment, and lower salaries, where I wouldn't be able to get a job without a work permit?" in response to some probing questions.

This did work, however, and customs released my stuff; it was delivered a few months after Christmas. I can now say I have all my items that were sent and can recommend the shipping company I used to people, as they did an excellent job of destroying the forest to properly wrap my belongings.

Getting Around

Dublin is a modern, compact city with multiple ways to get from one point to another. If you're renting a vehicle and driving, it does take some getting used to learning to drive on the left hand side of the road. Dublin also uses quite a few roundabouts for traffic, something many Americans are not used to using. Public transportation is a popular and efficient method of transportation such as the bus, Luas light rail, train, and the bike share service.

Leap
The Leap card can be obtained at numerous locations in Dublin, including the post office. A Leap card is a card that can be swiped to pay for mass transit in the city. Leap cards pay a slightly reduced rate on some of the transit options, versus paying directly with cash. To use the card, just swipe it at the clearly marked readers when getting on and sometimes off a mass transit service. To add funds, there are pay stations at Luas and DART stops. Or, if you're planning to use it often, you can set the card up online and add funds directly through the website, although the funds won't be reflected on your card until you swipe it at one of the station's machines. You can also just set up an auto top-up with your back account.

My experience with setting up the auto top-up was a frustrating experience following the directions on the website, which is poorly designed, but once it was setup, it is a handy system.

Luas

There are two Luas routes in the city. The Luas is a light rail
system, the Green Line that runs north and south and the
Red Line that runs east and west. Currently, the two lines do
not cross, but the city is in the process of extending the
Green Line so that it will cross over the Red Line.

The rates are based on the zones traveled in. A ticket can be
purchased at each boarding station. A day or multi-day ticket
is available. If using a Leap card, swipe the card at the station
when arriving and swipe it again after leaving the Luas. You
might or might not have to provide your ticket or Leap card
while on the Luas line. Transit police regularly board to check
and will write tickets for anyone who has not paid.

City Bus

The bus service runs quite regularly and throughout the
entire city and is a nice way to avoid driving in the congested
city traffic. To ride the bus, it is necessary to know your
destination when boarding the bus services in Dublin. You
will need to inform the driver where you plan to get off, and
they will charge you upon entry based on your destination. A
Leap card is a useful item to have when riding the bus. Upon
informing the driver of the destination, he or she will enter
the charge, and you can swipe the card for payment. If you're
paying with money, the buses only take exact coins. Before
getting on the bus, as you see them driving up, put your hand
out similar to flagging down a taxi to let them know you want
on; otherwise, the driver will continue on without stopping.

The buses have a red stop button that you can press to let
the drive know you want off, but you will notice that most
people hit the button and walk to the front prior to getting

off. I get the feeling that the driver won't wait long if you are getting out of your seat at the time he or she stops.

Unfortunately, Dublin bus drivers are notorious for having little regard for other people on the roads. There are exceptions, I'm sure. As of this writing, there is a YouTube video going around of a Dublin bus driver yelling and attempting to run a bicycle rider off the road. And personally, one of the times I rented a car, a bus driver forced me into the wrong lane, as he decided he wanted into mine, with no regard to me or the vehicle I was driving.

Along with the standard city buses, there are separate bus services that run to the airport—the Aircoach and Bus Eireann. Check the websites for schedules and rates.

DART Trains
The DART (Dublin Area Rapid Transit) lines are a convenient rail option to travel. They take the Leap card, run often, and are well maintained. They are also are a handy way to explore the coastal areas north and south of the city. The DART lines run from Howth and Malahide in the north to Greystones in the south with many stops along the way.

GoCar, Car Sharing
GoCar is Dublin's car sharing service, similar to ZipCar and other services in the US. A membership includes insurance and gas and allows users to reserve a car for short use from locations throughout the city.

Taxis

Taxis run all over the city of Dublin and are easy to flag down. All taxis in Dublin use meters, and most are pretty good about not driving around in circles to increase the fare.

For anyone with a smartphone, get the Hailo or Uber app. This app allows you to hail the closest taxi from the app and gives you an estimated time of pickup. The app also allows you to enter credit card information so that you can pay for the fare with the app. Currently, the Hailo app is only available for Android and iPhones, while Uber is available for the Windows phone as well.

Train

There are two stations located in Dublin. One is the Heuston Station on the western side of the city and the other is Connolly Station on the northeastern side of the city. Like many European countries, the trains are an efficient way to travel; they have modern cars and reasonable rates to transport users from one side of the country to the other.

Useful Links

DART	www.dart.ie
Dublin Bus	www.dublinbus.ie
Aircoach	www.aircoach.ie
Bus Eireann	www.buseireann.ie
GoCar	http://www.gocar.ie
Irish Rail	www.irishrail.ie
Luas	www.luas.ie

Owning a Vehicle

Getting a License

If you're planning on owning a vehicle, you will be required to obtain an Irish driver's license after one year. However, until that point, your US driver's license is considered acceptable. Even though you currently have a license, you will be required to first obtain a provisional driver's license, basically a learner's permit then you will be required to take the driver's test as if you're a new driver. Most cars in Ireland are manual transmissions, and if you take the driver's test in an automatic transmission vehicle, your license will not cover you for a manual transmission. So if you're looking to drive in Ireland, learn to drive a manual transmission.

To apply for a license, visit the motor taxation office, post office, or Garda station. Once you're there, you will be required to provide your PPS number, take an eye exam, and pass a written test. It is advisable to study for this test prior to applying, as the laws in Ireland for driving are different from the US. For example, no turns on red lights are allowed, as they are in the United States and many other countries. After passing the test, you will be provided a provisional license that is valid for two years, at which point you will be required to apply for a full driver's license.

After moving to Ireland, ask your Irish friends how many times they had to take the test, and rarely will you hear someone say only once. Many Irish drivers have to take the test multiple times before they are allowed to pass, and each time a fee is required. At the time of this writing, the fee per test is 85.00 euros.

Automobile Cost

The cost of owning a vehicle in Ireland is much higher than in the US and if obtaining a loan for the car, the interest rates are generally higher as well. On top of those costs, the government doesn't use its influence to force down the cost of fuel like in the US so petrol will cost more. Most vehicles are, however, much smaller than in the US so mileage is much better than what the average vehicle in the US gets. Insurance is required and is higher if you're driving on a provisional license. Also, a Pay Vehicle Tax (VRT) is paid when the car is purchased. If you're purchasing from a private owner, the fee can be paid at the Vehicle Registration Office, and motor tax is required. In Ireland, all these documents are required to be posted on the lower corner of the passenger side window.

Parking

Parking can be a pain in the larger cities such as Dublin, due to the number of cars on the road and the increasing population. Parking in lots or on the streets, the fees will generally be higher. The street parking does offer a pay by text service that allows people to pay for street parking with a mobile phone instead of a parking machine.

The parking police in Dublin are very strict and out constantly. Cars will regularly have their tires clamped, which will cost between 80.00 to 125.00 euros to have the clamp removed.

Driving

In Ireland and the UK, drivers drive on the left side of the road. This can take a little getting used to, and some of the signs are a little different. Speed is displayed in kilometers, and the rural roads around the country are narrow and can be a little stressful for someone who is from the US and is used to larger cars and wider roads. Beyond that, driving is not all that different. The lights mean the same, the gear shifter uses the same pattern even if being used by the left hand instead of the right, and it is recommended to avoid hitting pedestrians or bicyclists.

Speed limits are quite often enforced with radar and cameras with fines mailed to the home of the registered owner of the vehicle. Any traffic infractions will count as negative points on a driving record, which will affect the rates for automobile insurance.

Useful Links

Rules of the Road	www.rsa.ie
Department of Transportation	www.dttas.ie
Motor Tax	www.motortax.ie

Driving on the Wrong Side

Two months into my time in Ireland, it was time to move from my temporary housing into a permanent apartment. Although I didn't have a lot of belongings—a guitar some clothes, and other miscellaneous items—to move, there was still enough that a vehicle would be required, and possibly a of couple trips. Sure, I could have tried to talk one of my new coworkers into assisting me, and a few I'm sure wouldn't have minded much, but it felt a little rude. As fun as the idea of dozens of trips on mass transit sounded, along with hauling each item on my back, the idea was a little daunting. So, it seemed a good time to have my first right hand drive, left side road experience.

Knowing enough ahead of time that a vehicle might be needed at points, a GoCar sharing service was the perfect way to go rather than renting a vehicle for the day. Reserving the vehicle was easy enough through the website, although it was kind of messed up that they didn't have an app for my phone. At least at the time of this writing they didn't. I am going to assume that will be coming at a later date. But back to the story; the reservation process was quick—select location, pickup and drop-off time—and from there, I was good to go.

After swiping my GoCar card, which had arrived a few weeks earlier, across the pad on the windshield, I was let into the vehicle that the reservation told me was mine for the next few hours. The car was a small European brand I had never heard of prior to moving. It was white and had the GoCar logo painted across the side, so there would be no confusion as to what it was, and plenty of advertising for them as I drove down the road.

The first few minutes of driving from what would be the passenger seat were a little nerve-racking, not to mention the fact that I hadn't driven in almost three months anyway, the roads were more narrow, and the rules of the road just a little different. In Ireland, the UK, and a few other countries, they make jokes about the Americans driving on the wrong side of the road; of course, for those of us from the US, I would have to say driving on the left side of the road. The manual shifter being used by the left hand is the wrong side of the car. And most noticeable after pulling out into traffic, going from a larger American style vehicle to a very small fuel-efficient vehicle, I found that I was missing a good field of view that I had become accustomed.

When driving on the opposite side of the street first time, you literally have to fight the urge to turn into the wrong lane after a lifetime of driving one-way. And in doing so, you are so focused on staying on the correct side of the road that you have a tendency to miss a red light or two. At least in my case I did. It doesn't help that Ireland as a whole doesn't believe in using road signs and or any other legitimate method of marking roads, so it can also be a little discombobulating to try to find a route from one street to the next, especially when the GPS on your phone decides to lose its location connection due to the large old brick buildings that line the streets of Dublin. And, of course, when a GPS is needed, that is when it is not available.

Just stay behind this car, was often running through my mind down to my sweaty palms gripping the wheel of the little car. *If they are going, then that means this is one of the lights that I can go this way on.* Most Irish traffic lights are on the corners versus overhead; the walk isn't in sync with the traffic light. Often, it will say the walking traffic can go, but the vehicle traffic moving in the same direction can't. There is also a rule that I found out about later—you can't turn on a red light. Luckily, I did not find this out by a ticket showing up in the mail, as I did this often, but via friends informing me of the odd law.

I eventually did make it from the GoCar location to my larger company sponsored two-bedroom apartment outside of the city center and then to my new much smaller single bedroom apartment in the city. I only hit the curb twice, possibly ran three red lights, but luckily never turned into the wrong side of the road, although I really wanted to. An hour and a half later, the car was returned undamaged, and my first time driving in Ireland was complete. You would think after two months of not having a vehicle I would miss it, driving on the correct side of the road or not. But the reality is I didn't. It wasn't the stress of driving, as after a few other trips I'm now comfortable driving in the country. Having been a driver for over 20 years and with road trips, commutes, and the life of a vehicle owner that is required in the US, I have probably logged a million miles behind the wheel, if not more. So to now be able to commute via a light rail, walk to the store, and occasionally use a bicycle or car share to get around is fantastic.

Medical Care

The Irish healthcare system, unfortunately, isn't as good as many other socialized systems within Europe. Not to say that it is bad, but it's not as affordable as one would think. The system will be a dramatic change for anyone from the US, and the quality of care might not be considered up to the standards most Americans have become accustomed to. There are basically two choices for healthcare in Ireland. The first option is a work sponsored service provider, and the second is the Health Service Executive (HSE), which is the state sponsored system.

Health Service Executive allows anyone living in Ireland for at least one year to access HSE services. The cost of the services provided is based on an individual's income level.

Work sponsored healthcare is similar to what we are accustomed to in the US. This is where a set amount is taken out of your regular paycheck that goes to cover your insurance. One of the differences in Ireland, however, is that when you visit a doctor or other medical provider, you will need to pay the cost of the service up front. Then you will need to take the receipt from that and send it to your insurance provider to receive a payment for the service, deducting any amounts they don't cover. Based on personal experience, make sure that your doctor or dentist includes a detailed list of the services provided and the cost for each. When I mailed the paid bill to my provider, it just had the receipt and the total, which my provider denied it because it wasn't itemized.

Another difference between the US and Ireland is the wait times that will often be required for health services. In the US, we can usually contact our provider and get an appointment within a few weeks, potentially even less depending on the need. In Ireland, it is not uncommon to need to book an appointment months ahead of time for non-emergency services.

Emergency Care

If you're in need of emergency services or an ambulance, you can dial 999 or 112 from anywhere in Ireland. The ambulance will take you to the nearest public hospital with an emergency room to receive care. Note: There is generally a 100 euro fee for a visit to the emergency room. Check with your insurance provider to see if this can be reimbursed, as you will be expected to cover the cost out-of-pocket at the emergency room.

With public healthcare being available to all in Ireland, there can be a shortage of beds or long wait times when visiting an emergency room. It is recommended that if you are not in need of emergency care and can wait for a visit to your general practitioner, visit him/her instead.

Swift Care

Alternatives to emergency rooms at local public hospitals are the Swift Care services that can be used. Swift Care can be used for minor injuries such as breaks and sprains, minor burns, stitches, and other general medical emergencies. Note: Children under the age of 12 cannot be seen in a Switch Care and should be taken to a hospital emergency room instead.

Swift Care locations are not open 24 hours like emergency care facilities. The hours are from 8:00am to 10:00pm, seven days a week.

Check www.vhi.ie/swiftcare for locations, as well as what services are provided and what conditions cannot be treated at a location.

Pharmaceuticals

The Irish medical system is not as prone to solving issues with the use of medications as most American systems. It could be argued if this is good or bad, but the reality is that some medications that are easy to get in the US can be more difficult to obtain in Ireland. In some cases, medications that can be purchased over the counter in the US require a prescription in Ireland.

When traveling to other countries, it is common that similar medications can have different names. A couple of common ones are the US equivalent of acetaminophen in Ireland is paracetamol, and ibuprofen would be Nurofen or Solpaflex, although you can also by ibuprofen called ibuprofen. If you're confused, just talk to the pharmacist.

If you're moving to Ireland with an existing prescription, you will need to see a local doctor and have a prescription written. Irish pharmacists are not allowed to fulfill prescriptions from foreign doctors.

If you have a regular prescription, it is worth registering for the Drug Payment Scheme with the pharmacy. The scheme is a law that an individual or family is not required to pay more than 100 euro a month for prescription medications. This is a pretty good deal for anyone, such as seniors, who have to take medications regularly.

Hospitals
Hospitals in Ireland are similar to what an American would expect, with emergency services and other treatment services available at the locations. There are two different types of hospitals in Ireland. The first is publicly funded hospitals. These are either funded by the Irish government or the Health Services Executive. The public healthcare in Ireland makes services available to all citizens of the country. Yet, if you're traveling from the US or not an Irish resident, you would be expected to cover the full cost of a hospital visit. Because of this, it is recommended to have travel insurance if visiting or a local insurance provider if recently moving to Ireland. There are also private hospitals available for those with the money or insurance to cover visits.

Reproductive Health
Even with many of the recent changes in some states within the US restricting women's healthcare, Ireland is still a significantly more restrictive society due to the country's strong religious ties. It is possible to get the same access to birth control as in the US, but abortion is illegal throughout the country, regardless of circumstances. There have been pushes recently to change these laws due to situations of women dying because doctors would not provide an abortion even when a mother's health was in danger. As of right now, however, any women in need of abortions can go to England where there is a more liberal healthcare system. Fertility services are available through private clinics for anyone trying to conceive.

If you're planning to have a child or not planning but having one anyway, having a child is pretty much the same here as anywhere else. At least the baby comes out the same place anyway. The public healthcare system will assist with any needs and birthing of the child and will also assist with postnatal care up to six weeks after the birth. There are numerous OBGYN, midwives, and hospital accommodations to choose from throughout the country.

After your baby is born, his or her birth will be recorded at the hospital. If you choose private care or midwife service, you must register the birth within three months of the birth. As a US citizen, the birth must also be registered with the US embassy. Please be sure to take a copy of the Irish birth certificate to the embassy.

Useful Links

Ambulance	Dial 112 or 999
Department of Health	www.dohc.ie
Health Service Executive	www.hse.ie
Irish Health	www.irishhealth.com
Irish Medical Board	www.imb.ie
Swift Care	www.vhi.ie/swiftcare

Electric Meters

So let's say that every two months, you receive your electric bill. From the time you set up service and for the past six months living in your small one bedroom apartment, the bill averages about 45.00 euros a month. Then imagine when you receive a bill, which you expect to go down because it's moving into spring, that turns out to be 375.00 euros. Your first thought would probably be that it was an error of some sort and that a quick call to the electric company should hopefully resolve the issue.

After jumping through the usual hoops that are involved in calling into a call center, pressing the right numbers in the IVR, entering confirmation information, listening to the system tell me how much I owe, I eventually reached the human at the end of the line.

"Hi," I start off, "I received my bill, and it is for 375.00 euros. Normally, it is around 45 each month."

He takes a few minutes to review the bill and comes back with, "It looks like you called in a meter reading. And it looks like you used way more electricity than predicted."

"What do you mean predicted?"

He goes on to explain how the Irish electric system works. Each bill is an estimate based on past usage, and once every quarter someone comes around and reads the meter to get a usage amount. That bill gets adjusted based on the usage. In my case, since I live in an apartment this was the first time since I had been there that someone was able to actually read the meter. And I apparently had used way more electricity than they thought I would.

Of course, thinking to myself. I had run the electric fireplace quite a bit. Since the bill coming every couple of months was in a reasonable range, I figured my usage was fine.

"So, in Ireland it's not sent via any type of automated system. It's dependent on some random person going around and reading the meter? And if they can't read it, the amount I pay is based on an estimate? When they finally do get around to reading it, they just throw all those charges onto that next bill? So let's say I have no money in my account, and you send me a bill that is nearly ten times larger than I normally pay for two months usage on a tiny little apartment. I am stuck with it?"

"That is correct, but you can read the meter yourself and call in the meter reading to us."

"So, how do you know that I am sending an accurate reading if I am allowed to read my own meter? I could just call up and say that I've used x amount?"

"You could do that, but when they do get around to reading it that next quarter or whenever, it will get corrected."

"Okay," I chuckle thinking through the ridiculousness of this system. It's not just the fact that it is easy to scam the system, but also the fact that there is an entire staff of people roaming around the country reading meters—all of whom receive a salary, consume fuel in the vehicle they drive to do it, have pensions, and every other cost associated with being an employee. And, of course, all that cost goes onto the consumer, in this case me.

"I'm not sure where you are from," he continues, "but that is how it works here in Ireland. I could break the amount up into payments if that is a concern for you."

"No, I'm fine. It was just a little shocking to see when I received a bill so high, but I can cover it now that I know how the system works."

We end the conversation shortly after that, and that night when I went home I made sure to keep the heat off, instead bundling up in a flannel for warmth and throwing an extra blanket on the bed when I went to sleep. When I think of keeping the water tank on all night instead of turning it on in the morning like most people, I begin to see why many of the tanks in this country have that system.

If you are reading this book, please tell your friends to also buy a copy. I need the money because I don't like to wait for water to heat up in the mornings, although I don't mind bundling up in the evenings and reading by candlelight to balance it out.

Shopping

You know those massive grocery stores you are used to, those massive malls, and department stores? You can forget all about that in Ireland. Grocery stores, even the larger ones are much smaller affairs in Ireland. The stores are not only smaller in size, but also have a much smaller selection of goods. If you are a big fan of Cheez-It crackers or cheddar and sour cream chips, you might want to try to stock up before moving over, as you will have a hard time finding many goods easily available. The chips (crisps) selection is generally different brands of cheese and onion with a large selection of Doritos and Pringles mixed in.

Even though the selection is much smaller, there is still plenty to choose from in regards to the grocery stores; they have all the same meats and cheeses available, and since this is Ireland, you will never be at a loss for potatoes. Potato products go with every meal in Ireland. In recent years, with the influx of people moving to Dublin from around the EU, the choices have grown some and are continuing to grow as time goes on and people's tastes vary.

Be sure to bring your own shopping bag. This is an area where Ireland is ahead of the curve, as only a few cities in the US have passed laws charging extra for bags. In 2001, the Irish government passed a law charging an extra 22 cents per plastic bag if you don't bring one of your own or don't buy one of the cloth bags available.

Store hours will also be limited as compared to the US stores. You will be hard-pressed to find a 24-hour grocery store like it is easy to find in the US. Most late night shopping trips usually involve the Spar, a convenience store similar to 7-Eleven in the US.

In regards to retail goods, there are plenty of shops and stores to choose from selling all the same brands and goods available in any mall across the US. In central Dublin is Grafton Street. This is a popular destination for tourist and locals. The street runs north and south and is lined with restaurants and shops both local and places to pick up souvenirs. The street is closed to vehicles, and you can find buskers performing all year around.

North of the river is Henry Street. This is another foot traffic only street lined with department stores and shopping. Check out some of the side streets where you can find small farmers markets that sell fruits and vegetables.

Note: Clothing and shoe sizes vary between the US, UK, and mainland Europe. There is enough foreign traffic through the shopping stores so sales clerks can easily assist with converting sizes from US to European.

Things to Do and See in Dublin

There is a lot to see and do in a vibrant city like Dublin, so I am not going to go into a lot of detail on this subject. If you want to find out what to do, check out many of the numerous tour books available for purchase, websites, and the local populace who are always happy to share information. A website I would recommend subscribing to is Dublin Event Guide (see below for URL). They provide a weekly listing of events and other things to see in the city.

Useful Links

Castle and Garden Lists	www.castlesgardensireland.com
Dublin Tourism	www.dublintourist.com
Dublin Event Guide	www.dublineventguide.com
Heritage Ireland	www.heritageireland.ie/en/Dublin
Le Cool	http://lecool.com/dublin/en/current_issue
Volunteering	www.volunteer.ie

Top Ten Things to See in Dublin

Glasnevin Cemetery Museum
This massive cemetery is the resting place for numerous figures throughout Ireland's history, including the most visited grave of Michael Collins. There is also a small museum on the side.

The Guinness Tour
Visit the storehouse of Ireland's most popular beer and learn how to do a "proper pour" while you are there. You can also visit the Gravity Bar while on site and enjoy the view of Dublin.

The Old Jameson Distillery
Take a tour of the old distillery to learn about Ireland's most popular whisky. Note: When they ask for volunteers, be the first to raise your hand. Not everyone in the tours gets a chance to do a tasting.

Johnnie Fox's Pub
Hop onto the shuttle to Johnnie Fox's pub, one of Ireland's highest (altitude) and most famous pubs.

Kilmainham Gaol
Kilmainham Gaol is a former prison just west of central Dublin and a quick walk from the Luas Red Line. A tour of the prison includes a quick film on the history of the prison and an opportunity to explore the restored prison block and grounds. Films such as the 1969 version of *The Italian Job* and the 1993 film *Michael Collins* have scenes filmed in the prison.

Literary Pub Crawl
Actors perform pieces of work from Irish literary history on this walking tour through some Dublin pubs.

The National Museum
This is a great collection of Irish history and culture. Along with having a great exhibit, admission to the museum is free.

St. Patrick's Cathedral and Christ Church Cathedral
Named after Ireland's patron saint, the cathedral is the final resting place of Jonathan Swift. Outside the cathedral is a nice park area to sit and relax. A few blocks north of St. Patrick's is Christ Church Cathedral where you can see a mummified cat and mouse.

Phoenix Park
One of the world's largest urban parks, double the size of New York's Central Park, the park contains the Ashtown Castle tower, the remnants of a military fort, and is the residence of the Irish President.

Temple Bar
Wander the streets in Temple Bar, full of restaurants and so many pubs you won't be able to visit them all. My recommendation is to swing into the Porter House and try a pint of Brainblasta.

Top Ten Things to See in Ireland (Outside of Dublin)

The Aran Islands
A quick side trip from Galway, these three small islands are a lovely view into historic Irish life. Get off the boat, rent a bike, or just walk and enjoy the scenery.

Belfast
Visit Northern Ireland's largest city, where you can see the Titanic Museum and tour the streets to view the famous murals throughout the city.

The Blarney Stone
Lean back and give it a kiss if you want. Its powers are said to provide the gift of gab. The Barney Stone is located at Blarney Castle, which has more to see and do than just see and kiss the stone.

Kerry Cliffs
Not as dramatic as the Cliffs of Moher but with fewer visitors, a much nicer visit can be had.

Drive the Ring of Kerry
This scenic drive is a favorite among the Irish with its views and stops along the route. Plan a day or two and try to see it all. Don't wait on the weather, as it changes often.

The Giants Causeway
Not as large as you would think, this UNESCO World Heritage Site is well worth a visit to Northern Ireland.

Glendalough
Two lakes, hiking trails, and a monastic ruin offer a nice place to visit and walk around on a nice day.

Holy Cross Abbey
A restored monastery is still used as a place of worship and pilgrimage site.

Newgrange and Knowth
Constructed over 5,000 years ago, the monuments are older than Stonehenge. During the winter solstice, the sun will lighten the Newgrange passage to allow sun into the chamber during the shortest day of the year. The grass-covered mounds in Knowth are a pleasure to walk around in the summer.

Rock of Cashel
Sitting atop a hill in the town of Cashel, the Rock of Cashel offers a view of the surrounding country, the remnants of a monastery, and lovely little graveyard.

Pubs and Restaurants

If you like Irish pubs and bars, you will love living in Dublin. The city boasts numerous pubs, which offer a variety of whiskies, local beers including a properly poured Guinness, and standard Irish pub grub. As with many cities, restaurants and bars open and close regularly. As such, I will try to recommend locations that have been around for a while and don't look like they will be going anywhere soon. Be sure to check local listings for location status. The legal drinking age in Ireland is 18, and smoking is banned in restaurants and pubs.

The most consolidated set of pubs and restaurants is in the Temple Bar area. Located in the heart of Dublin's City Centre, Temple Bar is a collection of bars and restaurants with an occasional store. The streets are narrow cobblestone, and this is a must area for visitors looking for an evening out and a common stop for residents on a night out.

The majority of pubs allow people to bring children up to a certain time, usually around 8:00pm.

Note: Tipping isn't as customary in Ireland as in the US, so it is not expected to tip a bartender. It is, however, more common to tip a waiter or waitress, but in Ireland it isn't expected. Here, tips are actually for good service.

Twelve Pubs of Christmas

One thing I say regularly is pubs in Dublin are like Starbucks in Seattle—they have one on every corner. There is not a lot of difference from one to the other. Unlike Starbucks, at an Irish pub you will find an overpriced pint of beer instead of an overpriced latte and a friendly group of people to drink it with. A traditional Irish pub will usually have brick or dark wooden walls and a classic Irish feel to it. The best way to describe a proper Irish pub is to say that it is exactly like what you imagine an Irish pub to be.

Just like a classic Irish pub, the pub crawl is a time-honored tradition where the host will select a list of pubs and post the list on that classic communication tool of Facebook. From there the invite goes out with the schedule to participants to accept, decline, or forward along to other friends. From that point, it involves hitting each pub while trying to keep to the schedule as much as possible, with the knowledge that people can join and leave at any time throughout the crawl. The most serious and committed of crawlers participate from beginning to end. Most pub crawls limit the locations to only a few, generally three to six in a night, except for around Christmastime. At Christmas, in honor of the twelve days of Christmas, we have the twelve pubs of Christmas.

Twelve Pubs of Christmas - The invite read as follows:

> *List of Pubs: we will stick to the South Side and within decent walking distance!*
>
> *1) 4-4:50pm: Slattery's*

2) 5-5:45pm: Ryan Beggar's Bush

3) 6-6:45pm: Smyth's (Serves food)

4) 7-7.30pm: The 51, just across the street. Also do a dinner and pint for 10 euro, by the way, but that would need to be checked at Xmas!

5) 7:40-8:30pm: The Waterloo Bar & Grill (This one serves food too)

6) 8:45-9:30pm: Searsons of Baggot Street

7) 9.35-9:50pm: Henry Grattan

8) 10-10:50pm: Toners Pub (This one has both a cool beer garden and the best snug in Dublin 4)

9) 11-11:50pm: Doheny & Nesbitt

10) 11:50pm-1am: O'Donoghue's

11) 1am-till you drop: Baggot Inn next door (God forbid they let us in!!) or any club in town?

From my apartment, it was only about a ten-minute walk to Slattery's. The Saturday evening of this crawl was going to be a packed one I thought upon entering the venue. There were wall-to-wall people by the time I arrived, and it was only a little after 4 in the afternoon. To the right of the entrance was the bar, where my first goal was to get a pint of beer followed up by my second goal, which was to find anyone I recognized. The girl who had set up the pub crawl I knew from work, plus I had met a few of the others before. Beyond that, it was going to be mostly fresh people, since I had only lived in the city for six months at this point. After getting my beer and taking that first all-important sip, the one that always tastes better than any other with its freshly poured cold froth at the head, the search through the walls of people for my fellow pub crawlers began.

Working my way through the crowd body first to protect any possibility of spilling the beer, I found Adela, the one who set the event up. She was wearing a full-on Mrs. Santa outfit in honor of the event. I was the first to arrive she told me, and we began to talk about how crowded it was. Slattery's isn't far from Aviva Stadium, and, apparently, a rugby game had been going on early in the day, so the pub was full of revelers after the match, as well as others out enjoying the pub culture of the city.

"You know, what we need is some rules to go with the pub crawl. And every time someone breaks the rule they have to take a drink."

"Good idea."

The first rule of the crawl that we came up with was that at each pub we would have to decide on a rule for that particular pub, instead of coming up with them all at once. Plus, this would give others the chance to come up with ideas, alleviating us from doing all the thinking. As we were discussing this, one of Adela's friends arrived. He was Adela's housemate, whom I had met at a previous pub at some point for some event. It was, on occasion, difficult to understand him with his thick Italian accent mixed with the sound of the crowd.

Hanna was next to arrive. I had also met her previously and found her to not really be that friendly, so I didn't expect to spend much time talking to her. She was cute but snotty, in my opinion. She seemed to be in a little more of a festive mood on this occasion, also wearing a Santa hat, drinking a whiskey straight, and even offering me an extra Santa hat she had brought with her. So points to her for the whiskey drinking and hat.

"How about this," it was suggested at the second location, "we each order a shot of something, then pass it around five times and have to drink whatever shot is in front of us at the time." This task we attempted to perform while standing outside, as there wasn't enough room inside. In the process of passing around, one of the drinks was dropped. I ended up with a shot of whisky, which was easy to down in the little plastic shot cups, measuring about half the size of a standard one-ounce shot. After a quick check-in on Facebook to let people know where we were and to let my American friends know how awesome pub crawls in Dublin are, we were off to the next pub.

Pub three was across the street making for an easy commute. It was at this pub that I came up with the idea that we could only drink our drinks with our left hands. Whoever was caught using the right hand had to take a drink. Assuming I was being clever since I am a left-handed person, it quickly became apparent that cleverness was not to be my friend this evening. I got caught more than anyone using the wrong hand and ended up going through two pints before the next location. It was also at this pub more people joined the group, and the crowd grew larger.

From there, it was on to pubs four and five, with pub five being the one that had food and enough space to eat it—the Waterloo. Walking in, it was clear that the crowds were just as dense as the other pubs we had visited. There were wall-to-wall people, and we had to wait a long time at the bar for a drink. It was after ordering the drinks that we found the upstairs where the food was being cooked. They had a back patio with a barbeque setup and were doing burgers, hot dogs, and a vegetarian option. Hanna, one of the other people, and I found this out and ordered some food. Hanna was limited on choices for food since she was a vegetarian. I, however, being a meat eater didn't have any problem ordering the hamburger. Also upstairs, we found a table and a bar without a super long wait. You can tell how drunk a group of people is when you try to use logic on them when saying, "There is a table upstairs and a bar," and none of them move from the super crowded section downstairs.

Bar six was my least favorite stop on the list. As we attempted to work our way in through the people jammed near the entrance, which was impossible, there were two people crammed next to each other arguing. One was trying to leave, and the other was trying to enter; but due to a severe lack of crowd control, neither could achieve the task that they were intending. The only thing that seems to have prevented an actual fight from breaking out is, most likely, that the crowd was so jammed together, neither could raise an arm to throw a punch. Searsons was brightly lit, unlike most proper pubs, and severely overcrowded. It is the kind of place you read about in the news where a fire breaks out and people die because no one can get out. When a person reaches a proper point of drunkenness in the night, they don't want bright lights, white walls, and a clear view of whatever girl they are talking to. At least, I don't; most everyone else in the bar didn't seem to mind. It didn't help that the music was so loud it was impossible to have a conversation anyway. Near the bathrooms, we managed to find a bit of standing space, and someone was sent for the drinks at this location. Personally, I was counting down the minutes until the next pub, which took way too long to get to.

After leaving, the pub crawl moved from a set scheduled of stops to, "Where should we go next?" and "So-and-so is at such-and-such place. We should go there." In the end, we went to some bar that was more of a restaurant than a pub, but actually a pretty nice place. We continued the conversation we started early in the evening about the different stages of drunk.

"Irish drunk is the most drunk you can be," stated Adela, who isn't even Irish.

"Oh, come on," I responded. "It's borderline impossible to get drunk here with the tiny shots they use in mixed drinks and the low alcohol content in the beer."

"What? Irish people have a total reputation for being drunks."

"Sure, but that's apparently because they can't handle the alcohol. I've lived here for six months now and drink less now than I did in the US, where you can get a properly poured drink. By less, I'm saying quantity not regularity. Each social interaction usually involves alcohol. The reason it's harder to get drunk is because the quantity of alcohol in a drink is much less than in many other countries." I'm told this is to curb Irish alcoholism.

The debate went on as I received a text from a friend that asking if I would be joining him and his girlfriend where they were. His girlfriend was having a birthday party that evening, as well, and had texted about meeting up with them. Since the crawl was off track and people were all over the place, I suggested that we should move there, knowing nothing about it. And so, we were off to our final destination for the evening—Howl at the Moon, a dance club. This was my least favorite type of place to drink at. I can't dance. I like to hear the person next to me when talking. Even though I was only in my mid-thirties at the time, when it comes to dance clubs, I might as well be eighty in regards to my attitude about the people and location.

It wasn't long before Hanna, the only girl I had spent most of the evening talking to, left. Her cold attitude at first was beginning to wear off as we spoke throughout the evening and drank more, even after I went on a tirade about how terrible *Star Trek into Darkness* is, which she thought was a good movie. And so it was at this point, I began to think about heading home for the night as well. Sure, I might have stayed and started chatting up some random at the end of the night, a random who hadn't already identified who they were hooking up with for the night. The reality was I was tired, drunk, and being a cranky not-quite old man who wanted to leave. So I did. Being in Dublin, it was a nice cool walk home where I crashed for the night to wake up the next morning with a decent hangover.

The agreed upon stages of drunk:
- Sober - boring
- Merry - starting off well
- Tipsy - the person you are talking to is looking better
- Buzzed - a great place to be
- Inebriated - happy for the night
- Drunk/Pissed - time to stop drinking
- Sloshed - should have stopped drinking but too late to stop now
- Plastered - that embarrassing friend of yours
- Locked - stumbling around causing a scene
- Hammered - getting kicked out of bar
- Wasted/trashed - nausea and spinners
- Fucked - time to vomit and sleep next to the toilet
- Shit-faced - sleeping next to the toilet and not eating solid meals for the next few days
- Blackout drunk - waking up in an alley the next day wondering where your pants went
- Dead - describes itself
- Irish drunk - something the Irish people I was with said, because they think Irish are better drinkers than others . . . they aren't as previously referenced

Museums

Book of Kells and Library
See the famous book of Kells and the library above it.
*   Website: www.tcd.ie/Library/bookofkells

Dublin Writers Museum
Find books, letters, and personal items from Dublin's literary past.
*   Website: www.writersmuseum.com

Dublinia
Dublinia traces the story of Medieval Dublin from the English Invasion through the Black Death to the closure of the Monasteries in the 1540s.
*   Website: Dublinia.ie

Hugh Lane Municipal Gallery of Modern Art
Features modern and contemporary art.
*   Website: www.hughlane.ie

Irish Jewish Museum
The building was a former Synagogue built in the 1870's. The museum contains memorabilia relating to the Irish Jewish communities in Ireland.
*   Website: www.jewishmuseum.ie

The Old Jameson Distillery
Learn about whiskey making and more about this popular Irish whiskey.
*   Website: www.jamesonwhiskey.com

James Joyce Centre

Exhibition about this famous Irish writer.

- Website: www. jamesjoyce.ie

The Little Museum of Dublin

The History of 20th century Dublin in a small space.

- Website: www.littlemuseum.ie

Malahide Castle & Park

12th century castle on a 380 acre park. In the park is also a model railway museum and dollhouse museum.

- Website: www.malahidecastleandgardens.ie

Museum of Modern Art

If modern art is your thing, this museum is the place to go.

- Website: www.imma.ie

National Museum of Archeology & History

Artifacts dating back to 7,000 BC are on display as well as a good collection of Viking artifacts.

- Website: www.museum.ie

National Gallery of Ireland

Here you will find Irish art and European paintings.

- Website: www.nationalgallery.ie

Wax Museum

See famous people in wax.

- Website: www.waxmuseumplus.ie

Note: If I missed a museum worth mentioning, please let me know, and I will include it in later editions of this book.

Theatre

Dublin does not have as many live theatres for play productions as some cities, but the quality of the performances is almost always above par. Going to a local show is a great night out.

Live Theatre Listings:

Abbey Theatre
URL: http://www.abbeytheatre.ie/
Location: 26 Lower Abbey St, Dublin, DUBLIN 1

Gaiety Theatre
URL: http://www.gaietytheatre.ie/
Location: South King Street, Dublin 2

Gate Theatre
URL: http://www.gatetheatre.ie/
Location: Cavendish Row, Parnell Square, Dublin 1

The New Theatre
URL: http://www.thenewtheatre.com
Location: Temple Bar area

The Olympia Theatre
URL: http://www.olympia.ie/
Location: 72 Dame Street, Dublin 2

Lambert Puppet Theatre
http://www.lambertpuppettheatre.ie/
Location: 72 Dame Street, Dublin 2

Festivals:

Fringe Festival
The fringe festival runs from early September to the middle of September. The fringe festival generally promotes newer artists and productions.
URL: http://www.fringefest.com/

Dublin Theatre Festival
The Dublin Theatre is held in the fall from the end of September to early October.
URL: https://www.dublintheatrefestival.com

Check out
Entertainment and multiple theatre listings. Search by date or venue.
http://entertainment.ie/theatre/

Sports

Ireland has two distinctly Irish sports to offer the world. The first is Gaelic football, which is a combination of soccer and football, or European football and American football, depending on your version of the naming. Players can touch the equivalent of a soccer ball with their hands, bounce it, and can kick it in the goal for more points or over the goal for fewer points. The game is high speed and isn't just a bunch of guys running back and forth on the field pretending to be injured like the other well-known game revolving around ball and very few points.

The other distinctly Irish game is hurling. This can only be described as field hockey meets baseball and soccer. Players use a stick called a hurley, which is similar to a small hockey stick that could also double as a weapon used to break heads open in battle. The players attempt to use the hurley to hit a baseball sized ball down the field or run with the ball on the hurly to score points by hitting it into a goal.

Both of these games are very intense and brutal with players playing past injury. Only in the last few years have helmets been required of the players in this sport.

Rugby and soccer (football in Europe) are also very popular sports in Ireland, with the World Cup being the only thing people talk about every four years. Most of the top Irish players go play for English football teams, so it is not common for the Irish team to make it into the World Cup with most Dubliners rooting for a favorite team from another part of the world.

For American football lovers, there are a few pubs that will show games. The Super Bowl is also a popular event for expats in Ireland. The Woolshed next door to the Cineworld is a popular place to watch a lot of sports, including American football on Sundays. The bar has multiple floors, with numerous TVs and screens to watch games on.

If you're looking to participate in sports, there are numerous golf courses in the country, as well as plenty in the UK to travel to and play on. Of course, there are also local soccer fields and teams, as well as hurling and rugby teams. Ice hockey, baseball, and basketball fans will have a harder time finding local places to participate.

Outside of Ireland

A great advantage of living in Dublin over anywhere in the US is having the option to hop on a flight for a relatively short distance to the rest of Europe. You can actually make a statement like, "Let's go to London this weekend," and do it for under 100 euros and a one-hour flight.

There are dozens of travel guides and internet resources for advice on where to go, what to do when you get there, and where to stay. Here is some generic advice to make your trip more pleasant.

Hop-On Bus Tours
Most major cities in Europe are considered tourist destinations, and most have hop-on hop-off buses that run throughout the city. These are nice when it comes to a city you have never been in and want to see the sites. The buses usually stop at most of the major tourist sites and run regularly. They also generally are open top, so on nice days it's a great way to relax and snap pictures of sites as you move past them.

If you're only going to be in town for a single day, these might not be a worthwhile investment depending on where you are. The buses tend to be a little slow as they can get stuck in traffic and stop regularly. In London, for example, the traffic is very dense, and it is possible to pay for the ticket to see a couple of the sites, and have spent most of your day. My advice is to plan in advance a couple stops on the bus to get off at, see those, and cruise past the others.

If you are going to be in town for a couple of days, which most people are, use the same process of visiting a few of the stops on a hop-on bus, then the next day in town and walk or taxi to the other sites.

In Belfast, I found the buses to not run as regularly as they stated, and at one point I had a driver drive right on past me without stopping. This can be very frustrating if you have a limited time in the city, as over an hour at a stop is not the best way to spend a day. Disregarding this incident, however, I would highly recommend the hop-on buses. My experience has been that these are a great way to see the main tourist destinations in a new city and allow me to check many of these sites off my to-see list. I also have a better idea of the layout of a city and can plan my next trip. As I mentioned, flying throughout Europe from Dublin isn't even remotely close to the cost of flying to Europe from the US.

Some of the buses also offer a multi-day ticket; this might be worth the investment in the larger cities with more to see and worse traffic.

Multi-Site Tour Tickets
In some cities, you can purchase tickets for multiple tourist sites at once, rather than purchasing each location one at a time. Usually, these allow for a bit of a discount on the overall cost. For example, in New York (I know not a European country), a book can be purchased that has many tickets into many of the major sites in the city. Some of these tickets allow holders to bypass some of the longer lines. Edinburgh also offers these options when visiting the castle and a few other sites. These can be purchased by the ticket agents at many of the sites. The disadvantage to this is if you

don't visit all of the sites, you might be out a few euros, pounds, or dollars. But if you do visit them, you will have saved money and potentially time. Do some online research or read a tour book prior to your trip to find such deals.

Irish Whisky Tour

This is Ireland, after all, and beer and whiskey are as Irish as potatoes and talking about the weather. So why not take a whiskey tour while you're in the country? Start the tour off in Dublin before moving west out of the city for about an hour to visit three distilleries in a short distance from one another. The tour then moves southwest then back up.

The Old Jameson Distillery
The Jameson Distillery is a popular tour stop for anyone visiting Dublin. Tours run seven days a week and last about an hour. Visitors are provided the opportunity to sample the Jameson brand, and a select few are chosen to partake in a tutored whiskey tasting.
- www.jamesonwhiskey.com

The Kilbeggan Distillery
Established in 1757 the Kilbeggan Distillery is the oldest licensed distillery in Ireland. Multiple daily tour options are available; visit the website to book in advance.
- www.kilbegganwhiskey.com

Locke's Distillery Museum in Kilbeggan Co
The museum is a view into the old Locke's Distillery, which is no longer distilling whiskey. The museum is open daily.
- www.classicwhiskey.com/distilleries/lockes.htm

Tullamore D.E.W.
Founded by Daniel E. Williams, this is located on the site of the original distillery the visitor center. The guided tour walks visitors through the history of Tullamore D.E.W., including a

tasting of the whiskeys. The site also provides food and makes for an excellent stop for lunch.

- www.tullamoredew.com

The Dylan Whisky Bar

Continuing south from Tullamore, there are multiple hotels in Kilkenny that make for a nice place to stay after a day of whiskey sampling. Located in Kilkenny and not a distillery, the Dylan is a Victorian style bar that contains roughly 100 of the world's finest whiskies.

- www.thedylanwhiskybar.com

Jameson Experience, Midleton

If you want to continue southwest, you will find the Midleton Jameson Experience. Previously the Old Midleton Distillery similar to the Jamison tour in Dublin, guided tours last about one hour and end with a whiskey tasting.

- www.jamesonwhiskey.com

Old Bushmills Distillery

Located in the northern tip of Northern Ireland, it is advised to call the distillery in advance to verify they are open for tours.

- www.bushmills.com

Cooley Whiskey Visitor Centre

Located in Northern Irelands Cooley Peninsula, the pub has regular tastings and a visitor center to learn more about Cooley Whiskey.

- www.cooleywhiskeybar.com

Note: Please use good judgment when whiskey tasting and if choosing to drive.

Motorcycling the Wild Atlantic Way

Day 1

We peered out of the window to get an idea of what our first day on the road was going to be like, and we could see the weather was looking fantastic for our first day on the motorcycles. The sun was shining, and even though there were a few clouds in the sky, none of them looked like they were planning to release any precipitation on the world below. We finished cramming our gear into our bags and piled everything into the trunk of a cab for the commute to the northwest side of Dublin and the office of Celtic Rider, the agency we were renting the bikes from. Chris and I had been talking about doing a motorcycle trip for a few years by this point, but the trip had always been planned as a US trip. That was until my relocation to Ireland changed the plans. One day, I had the idea that instead of me flying back to the US, he should fly over to Ireland for a ride around my new country of residence. Of course, that was a hit with the young man who had never left the US borders at this point in his life. So with some planning and scheduling, we arranged seven days on the road at the end of September.

Chris was a novice rider having only had his motorcycle license for a short time and not a lot of hours on an actual motorcycle. But we read through the requirements of renting a bike, which pertained to age and time with a license, but nothing about how many miles a person had to put on a motorcycle of their own. Chris was young, early 20's, and much taller than I, so I wasn't worried about his physical ability to handle the motorcycle. With his lack of experience on extended rides or riding in Irish traffic, I was a little worried about his safety. Plus, there would be the weather to concern ourselves, and the roads in Ireland have a reputation of not being the best. But, once the trip was booked, we were committed. I scheduled the bikes for three days after he arrived to give him time to get over his jetlag and adjust to the time difference. I couldn't do anything to help with his experience levels, but I could at least make sure he was awake while on the bikes, as I would have preferred to send him intact and unharmed back to his girlfriend in the States.

At Celtic Rider, the guys had out motorcycles ready to go as we arrived. Mine was a blue 2010 BMW F650GS, and Chris was on a 09 version. I was hesitant on renting these particular bikes, as I previously owned a blue 2010 F650GS, and it spent more time in the shop being worked on than it did on the road. I know BMWs have a reputation of being reliable, but my personal experience with one was the complete opposite. Out of other choices, we decided they fit the bill for what we needed to ride around Ireland in seven days—light enough for Chris to handle and not too much power but enough if it was needed. They each had panniers and plenty of storage for our gear. Plus, they were factory lowered with the lowered seat as well to allow my short ass the ability to reach the ground.

The guys went through the paperwork with us, offered a map of the country, and did a quick walk around the bikes, giving Chris a closer tour of the bikes. BMW uses an odd system for turn signals on those bikes that other manufactures don't use, so it was good for him to take some extra time on it. A quick change into our riding gear and loading of the bikes, and it wasn't long before we were off. At least I was off; Chris had his first bike drop in the parking lot as he was leaving. I tried to warn him that the bikes were more top heavy than what he was used too, but the only way I've found to learn about that from experience is to drop a bike or two. I knew at some point he would probably drop the bike, and better in a parking lot with no traffic than on the road. Although, I would have preferred a different parking lot than the one we were renting our bikes from. The bike had clearly been dropped a time or two before so it didn't look like he added any additional scratches to the panniers.

Originally, the plan was to do a southwest route around the country and move our way up the west coast and back. But since the rental place was on the northwest side of Dublin and after seeing Chris looking nervous, I decided to switch the route around and go counter clockwise instead. This way we could avoid the congested roads and the city of Dublin in order to stay on quiet, slower roads, giving him a chance to get more familiar with the bike before working our way into more traffic. We decided to make our last stop now our first and went to Newgrange monument.

We arrived around 2:00 in the afternoon due to our slow pace, primarily at the hands of Chris nearly falling over every time we stopped or killing the bike at each start, to find out that we had a few options. The first was at 3:15 to see Knowth, a lesser-known monument at the location, we could wait until 4:45 to see Newgrange, or, of course, we could see both. Waiting for Newgrange would have us leaving the site after 6:00pm, and we still wanted to get some more distance between us and Dublin before finding a place to sleep for the night. Knowth seemed worth seeing and even though not as well-known as Newgrange, still worth a visit. Both sites are passage tombs older than Stonehenge. So we bought our tickets and grabbed a quick bite to eat before loading ourselves along with the other tourists on the stuffy shuttle bus. The shuttle bus dropped us off at the site where we followed the group still wearing our full motorcycle gear of heavy pants and boots and carrying our thick jackets.

Knowth is a lush green series of man-made mounds and is the largest of the passage graves in the area, even larger than its more well-known neighbor of Newgrange. From what we could hear from the guide who was drowned out by the blowing wind as she spoke, the site went through many iterations over the years from burial site to small fort to big round hills that people didn't know housed anything before being rediscovered again. The history of the place, as it is known is documented well enough, and getting a chance to view and wander around the site was worth more than hearing about it.

From there, we headed northwest with a few random stops along the way before finding the pleasant little town of Castleblaney. As we rolled into town and parked the bikes in our search of a B&B or hotel for the night, a man walks up to us. "How do you like the bikes?" he says.

"So far so good," was my response. "Are you from around here?" I asked. "We are looking for a place for the night. Any recommendations?"

"Right around the corner here is a B&B," he pointed, "and if no one is there, the owner runs that bar down there." He pointed, "You should be able to find someone there."

The conversation led into our route, and he asked to see our map. We hadn't planned anything out on the map, but he looked anyway with a series of suggestions of things to see on the "Wild Atlantic Way," a road that runs down the west coast of Ireland.

"Just follow the signs; it's very clearly marked as you work your way."

The man, it turned out, was a motorcycle rider as well and had ridden all over the country. A buddy of his and he were going to be taking their bikes down to Northern France the following week for a road trip through Normandy and other north coast sites. It sounded like a great trip. I could tell he wanted to talk motorcycling, but after our first day's ride, I was ready to get a room and relax a bit. We said our goodbyes, and I walked over to the B&B to find a room while Chris stayed with the bikes.

After checking in to our little shared room, Chris showered to wash the nervous sweat off from his first day on the bikes, while I placed a quick call to check in with a loved one and let her know we hadn't died. Then we headed out for a much needed pint and food at a local pub. It started to rain as we walked. Not bad timing.

Day 2

"You lads want the full Irish?" the man asked us when we walked down the loud old wooden stairs of the B&B to the breakfast room.

"Sure," we responded.

He pointed to a table that was already set with juice, cereal, and yogurt.

"Tea or coffee?"

We both responded with tea and sat down with our phones to look at the route we wanted to take. The plan was to visit the Giants Causeway on this trip, but in looking at the map, calculating how long it would take to get to the northern end of the island, how long it took us just to get where we were, and really wanting to focus the trip on the west coast, we decided to follow the advice of the guy we had talked to the previous night and head to Donegal. Then we would follow the Wild Atlantic Way down the west coast from that point. It was at this point that the food arrived—meat with sides of meat, egg, beans, lots of toast, and potato.

"Oh, you should eat that," I say pointing to the black pudding. "You'll love it."

"What is it?" Chris asked.

"I'll tell you after you eat it."

He takes a bite, makes a face showing that it wasn't disgusting but not good either.

"It's blood sausage or black pudding. The first time I had it on the menu, and it was written 'black or white' pudding with the breakfast; so I was like, 'Sure I'll try the black pudding,' thinking it was similar to a chocolate pudding in the US. Turns out, it wasn't."

After the fullest Irish breakfast I have ever had since moving to Ireland and Chris' first, we walked to the lake and park that was near the B&B where I snapped a few pictures of the scenery and some pictures of a couple abandoned buildings.

Even though we managed to avoid the rain again, there was nothing we could do about the wind, and the ride wasn't so much a ride for the joy of it. Instead, it was a ride to hold on for dear life as we hauled ass down the highway with cross winds battering us from both sides. This wasn't helped by the fact that we spent a large portion towards Donegal on the highways instead of the back roads, which were much more fun. Not only was I worried about myself getting blown over, I was really worried about Chris overcompensating for a gust of wind off a passing truck and ending up rolling along with his bike down the road. But he held up, and we made it to our destination without any casualties.

We arrived in Donegal a little after 5:00 in the evening and were able to swing by the tourist office to get assistance from one of the most helpful tourist office personnel I had ever met. She must have been in her mid-30's, a little overweight, and not the best looking girl; but when it comes to tourist office assistance, she had hotel recommendations, places to eat, and found us a nice B&B in the middle of town with off street parking for the bikes that was just perfect. After checking in to the B&B and grabbing some food, we ended the night at a local pub with local music and locals to talk to, enjoying the evening that lasted late into the night. We were drinking whisky and beer with a local whose son was rocking out in a wheel chair on the dance floor with a local women's soccer team who had shown up by that point.

Before I close out day two, I feel I must call out an unfortunate casualty we experienced while on the highway into town. My one-week-old phone that was being used for its GPS navigation went flying out of the mount that attached it to the handlebar and ended up in pieces all over the road. I think I didn't lock it in place properly, so when we hit the 120 KPH max speed, it wasn't long before it shook out of place, bounced off my leg on the way down, and landed on the pavement. It was driven over a few times before I was able to scrape up the pieces in the hopes of finding the SIM, which was the only piece I couldn't find.

Day 3

Our first rain day was waiting for us as we loaded the bikes. But it wasn't long before the rain cleared up and the roads dried out, as we were able to enjoy some of the best riding so far traveling south along the coast following the squiggly line directing us along The Wild Atlantic Way. Without a proper navigation system, we didn't have much of a choice other than to follow the signs, or occasionally stop, pull out the old school map, and pick a point on the route to see. This actually worked out really well, and I'm sure it allowed us to see stuff we might not have otherwise. The ocean, the pastures, and the scenery were fantastic. We only made a few stops for photos, including the gravesite of WB Yeats and the cathedral near it. Evening arrived as we reached our destination of Westport. The little town dubbed the "cleanest town in Ireland" has a little river flowing through it with narrow streets of shops, B&Bs, and, of course, restaurants. We did a little searching and found a place to stay for the night with parking. It was a little outside the center of town, which we didn't care for; but the people were nice, and we could leave the bikes safely in front of the house.

Day 4

It turned out the B&B was not as nice as we had hoped. Being a little outside of town, one might think that we wouldn't have a lot of noise to deal with. Unfortunately, since it was a little out of town, there was a dog in the back barking at the wind for most of the night. The room itself didn't have any heat in it, and in fact was a few degrees cooler than the cold night air outside. And best of all, the morning shower didn't have hot water. There was a number on the key they left us to call, so I called it and received a generic message that the phone was off.

Not being able to reach anyone at the number, walking the building and not finding another living person, and feeling they didn't provide all the services agreed upon for the rate, we left 40 euros on the counter instead of the agreed 80, along with a note saying, "No heat in the rooms, no hot water in the shower, and no one answering the phone at the number on the key. Since we received half the services, you receive half the rate." It was a fair deal in my mind. From there, we lucked into a nice patch of sun for the ride to Galway, and after a few stops to photograph some sheep in a field, we made it into town early, grabbed some lunch, checked into the room early, and decided to spend the rest of the day off the saddle walking the town, followed up by a visit to the hotel's gym, pool, and hot tub to relax for the rest of the day.

Day 5

The Irish gods of weather were on our side as we left the lovely hotel in Galway for a lot of riding and a lot of stops. The wind was calm, the rain stayed away, and even though the sun never really cleared behind the clouds, it did its job of keeping us nice and warm as we cruised down the roads to take pictures of cows, old abandoned castles and churches, and the famous cliffs of Moher, or really the tourist of Moher. Pulling into the massive parking lot, we paid the parking fee, parked the bikes, and locked the helmets to the bikes. I grabbed my camera to take some pictures of this famous natural wonder that many websites have list of top ten things to see in Ireland. You might have noticed it's not listed on my top ten list. Following the crowds, we worked our way to the visitor center for a quick piss break and to check out the display of the history of the area and, of course, some of the shops selling all kind of trinkets for the traveler to purchase. From the shop, there is a wide path crowded with visitors leading up to the sides of the cliffs. To the left side of the cliffs, there was a long walkway lined with travelers taking selfies and pictures of family members on the edge of the high cliffs or pictures of the cliffs off to the right. And to the right, there was a tower and more long walkways lined with visitors taking more selfies or swapping cameras with other tourists to take turns photographing each other.

The cliffs are a fantastic site to see, and there is a little excitement as you stand looking over the sides as far as you dare to go, waiting for a gust of wind to rush up and blow the person next to you off the cliff, as they were more daring or dumb and felt safe enough to walk or crawl all the way to the edge for a sit or stand. After taking a few selfies of our own, we carried ourselves, jackets, heavy pants, and boots we were wearing all the way back to the parking lot, being made heaver with the sweat we were soaking into the clothing in the warm late summer weather.

Taking the back roads led us down some narrow lanes, the kind that you hear about when people describe the roads of Ireland—where there is just enough room for one vehicle, and you hope that the one coming in the opposite direction isn't doing the posted 100 KPH.

While stopping in some town and looking at the GPS on the phone, a kid on a bicycle challenged me to a race, which I politely informed him that I'd probably win even with the panniers on the bike. At this point, his friend joined in the conversation, and we had a nice discussion on the cost of the bikes, how much to rent one, and whether or not I would let him take mine for a ride; I declined. When cruising around on a motorcycle, it invariably leads to conversations with other travelers, even those not on motorcycles.

On this day as we crossed the river on a little ferry, a man came up to ask us if the bikes were rented (which they clearly are, as identified by the stickers all over the bikes). As it turned out, he was over from Seattle, a small world to run into someone from the same city as mine.

After the ferry, we stopped into the little town on the other side and checked into the Ferry House, the first B&B/hostel we found. From there, it was out to the Swanky, a local. And this is the most local I've experienced so far. Upon walking in, we were face-to-face with a couple dozen guys and two girls, all of whom went silent when we entered, gave us a look, and then went back to the conversations they were having. We prayed not to get food poisoning as we ordered our meals from the Swanky, along with a couple pints. The food didn't provide us with poisoning, and mine was pretty decent tasting. The beers were cold and yummy, and we ended up staying later than most of the locals almost closing out the pub at 8:30 after the rest of them had gone home for the night.

Day 6

Stopping near the end of the Ring of Kerry in a little town called Sneem, which appears to be set up only for the purpose of selling stuff, food, or accommodations to tourists, we do what we have been doing at each nightly stop—find a B&B to check into for the night. On the main street, there are a couple, so I walk into the first one and ask for the rate. A short angry looking woman who didn't seem too interested in renting a room to a couple of guys covered in motorcycle gear quoted me 30 per person, so I then check at the one down the street, and they are offering the same rate. I'm sure this was coordinated in advance between the two for competition purposes. However, the second place seems more friendly, responding to my question of, "How are you?"

with, "Much better now that you are here," and offers a
place off the street for the motorcycles; so we choose it.

The day started off from Tarbert where we stayed the
previous night and received one of the largest full Irish
breakfasts of the trip so far. We enjoyed three types of meat
including sausage, Irish bacon, and, of course, blood sausage.
This was all accompanied by an egg, hash browns, a bowl of
beans, toast, cereal, yogurt, and, of course, orange juice and
tea to wash it all down. I felt a little bad leaving so much food
on the table when we were done, but we are only two
people and neither of us able to finish it all.

We managed to add a lot of miles to the bikes hitting over
600 total for the trip by this point, and this being the most
miles added in a single day. Our goal for the day was mainly
to reach the Ring of Kerry, so the fact that we are about done
with it put us ahead of plan. That's even counting the times
we got off the ring to check things out like some cliffs that
personally I found more interesting than the Cliffs of Moher,
primarily due to a much fewer tourist population, stops at
some abandoned cathedrals and other sites, and, of course,
food and bathroom breaks.

We continued to follow the Wild Atlantic Way south on some
narrow yet very well maintained roads with some fantastic
riding that I would have loved to get with the GoPro if the
battery hadn't died by that point. But who cares if that
worked; what's important is the bikes ran great, and Chris
didn't drop his at any point. The scenery was beautiful, and it
was hard not to stop as often as I wanted. But with the fine
weather and the winding roads, it was only my body that
forced me to stop for the night, not my desire to continue

riding down the lovely west coast of the country with its green fields of pastures full of cows and sheep and the Atlantic Ocean on the other side. This is the part of motorcycle riding that I love, and non-riders just don't understand. Sure, there is extra danger in being on a bike, but with that comes a freedom—a freedom of the wind blowing against you and the connection you feel to the world around that can't be obtained while wrapped in a metal and glass box. Instead of rocking out to the music or texting a friend on the phone with the air conditioning on high, you are alone with your thoughts and the heightened awareness that gives you the ability to relax and enjoy the feeling of the bike winding smoothly through the turns and the sound of the engine as it revs up coming out of the turns. The sky is bluer, the wind is crisp, and the looks of the cows and sheep more distinct.

Day 7

We leave our odd little B&B for what will hopefully be the last B&B of the trip, not that there was anything wrong with this one, even though the toilet involved a walk down the carpeted hall past the room with a young couple who was touring the country by car. The shower for our use was in their room. And by in their room, I don't mean separate room adjacent to the bedroom, but actually in their bedroom, forcing us to coordinate our showers in the morning. We had to make sure one was out of the room at the time the other was showering. Yet, I will say that even though the shower was in a bedroom, at least it had hot water. I will also say the proprietor of this particular B&B was one of the friendliest we had come across so far. His friendliness extended after we checked in, as well with him always checking to make sure we were fine after showing us the little room and pointing out the tea was their own special blend they came up with about three years ago. He and his wife were the epitome of what one would expect from a B&B—friendliness, food, and an offer of guidance on things to see as we moved along.

The sun was in our eyes, the roads were void of traffic, and another nice day of riding awaited us as we rolled the two BMW's out of the fenced driveway they had spent the night in.

As we pulled away from the little town that appeared to be designed with the tourist in mind, we headed towards Cork, a well-known town in the southwest of Ireland that seems to be the reference point people ask me about when I mention this trip. We made our first stop at an abandoned church overgrown with shrubbery and surprisingly devoid of graffiti. I could see that Chris was getting a little tired of the site of abandoned churches and ancient graveyards, so after a few pictures of the church and a few of the sheep in the pasture near, we moved on down the road for a few hours before having a nice lunch in a little café, followed up by road, and more road. Then we hit the traffic of Cork and signs that we were on our way back to the real world after such a nice trip. Into Cork, we wanted to swing by Blarney Castle not so much to see and kiss the stone, but for the castle itself which is historically significant and really impressive even today. We did, however, pay our 12 euros, climbed the stairs to the top of the castle, and kissed the stone as so many thousands before us, not in the hopes of picking up the gift of eloquence that it offers, but mostly in the hope of not picking up some nasty mouth virus.

"Congratulations," I joked as we worked our way down the narrow circular stairwell of the castle. "My herpsypholites has been passed to you at kissing the stone after me."

I actually did feel a little gross after touching my lips to the discolored rock that millions have lipped before me and promptly used the bathroom sink in the restrooms to wash my face and spit a little.

From there, we planned to stay in Cork but heading back into town all we really found was traffic and congestion; we made a quick decision to head over to Middleton to stay for the night. I had wanted to swing by the distillery in town, but by the time we worked our way out of town during the rush hour evening commute and found a hotel, the distillery had closed for the night. So all we really could do was find some food, have a quick drink, and relax for a few hours before attempting to sleep in one of the loudest hotels in the country, or at the least loudest on our trip. My theory is that when they were building the place, they forgot to add insulation into the walls. We were able to hear the person in the room next to us take a piss each time they went to the bathroom, which they did often, and the sound of each door in the hallway as they slammed shut from people entering or exiting.

Day 8 and Back to Dublin

The guys at Celtic Rider were glad to see us as we rolled into the parking lot, not just because they probably saw Chris drop his bike the day we picked them up, but because we were a day late at returning them thanks to a slight miscalculation on my part. I had called them the previous day to let them know we would be late, and they were understanding. I had explained that we were just having too much fun to return them on time, and, of course, I would be willing to pay for the extra day.

Returning to Dublin was the epitome of bittersweetness with the trip being at its end. It would be nice to sleep in my own bed and eat something besides the standard Irish breakfast in the morning. However, our fantastic trip was over. The bikes were back at the rental agency with 939 total miles added to the clocks and undamaged. With that, no more winding roads, no more random stops at historic sites, and no more of the freedom and relaxation that comes with the feeling of being on the open road with two wheels underneath you.

Tips for Your Trip

You don't have to be on motorcycles to enjoy a trip like this. If your preferred method is a car, go for it. On our trip, the mode of travel was a key part in our plans, but if the sites are yours, get out and do it. Whatever your mode of travel is, here are some tips for such a trip.

1. Turn the GPS off. GPS is going to choose the most efficient and quickest route to get to a destination. But sometimes, it it fun to go off the beaten track and see what you find. You don't have to drop yours on the side of the highway as I did, but if I hadn't, it is possible we might not have seen the rock covered landscape of the Burren or the Kerry Cliffs. They were not as dramatic as the Cliffs of Moher but much less traveled.

Both of which we probably wouldn't have seen if we hadn't accidently turned down a road and decided to follow it to see where it went. You can always turn the GPS back on later if you want.

2. Don't book rooms in advance. This will free you up to take detours and not worry about getting to a destination at a specific time. There are B&Bs approximately 15 to 20 minutes from anywhere you are in Ireland. They might be inconstant in services, but they will always provide a bed to sleep for the night and breakfast in the morning.

3. Don't forget soap, toothpaste, and a pen. Not all B&Bs provide soap, and you will be surprised as to how often you might need a pen or pencil.

4. Always have cash on you. We had a running joke at each stop as to how much something was going to cost to see, and the joke was that it was going to cost 12 euros. It didn't always, but almost always it was 12 euros.

5. The roads are not that bad. Ireland has this reputation of having terrible roads, narrow and in poor condition. If we did this trip on motorcycles with no problems, so can you.

6. Take lots of pictures, and take your time. You might not see all Ireland has to offer, but you will appreciate what you do see and experience by not jumping out of your car, snapping pictures, then hopping back into the car to the next photo stop.

7. And most importantly, ignore what your mother told you and talk to strangers. The Irish are a friendly people, so sit down on a stool at the pub near your B&B and have a conversation with a random person you will never see again. It will be worth it.

Terms and Slang

US English	Irish English
Chips	Crisps
The cabinet	The press (ex. "The candy is in the press.")
The commuter bus	The feeder (slang)
Elevator	Lift
Flashlight	Torch
Fanny (term for a person's rear area)	Fanny (term for girl's front area) = jumper = sweater
The John = The Men's Room	The Jacks
Pudding (delicious creamy sweet substance)	Pudding (sausage disk thing that is not delicious, sweet, or creamy) They do have pudding, but it is apparently just called sweet dairy product.
Season	Series
Vacuum	Hoover
What's up, or how's it going?	What's the craic? (has nothing to do with narcotics)

In Summary

The grass is always greener on the other side, and our ideas on what we think living in another country is like versus the reality doesn't necessarily always match. In Ireland, the grass is really green thanks to the weather. It has many of the same problems first world countries experience, such as politicians poorly managing tax money, congested traffic, and too many people. It also has some third world problems, such as an outdated electric grid, a major airport without a rail system connecting it to the city, and politicians poorly managing tax money. Ireland is the first place I've experienced that falls into the second world country category. It has the problems and benefits of first and third world countries all combined into one. But when it comes down to it, the benefits far outweigh the problems.

I hope anyone reading this didn't choose to live in Dublin or travel to Ireland for financial reasons. As you have read through this, you probably came to the realization that it's not a cheap place to live. What makes living in Ireland great, however, is the people and the experiences. It is a cliché to say, but the truth of the matter is the experiences we have when visiting other countries is what makes society better as a whole.

Throughout generations, India and Pakistan have been conflicting neighbors. At work, there was a guy from India who found out that we would be hiring a guy from Pakistan. He was hesitant at the idea of having the Pakistani sitting next to him. And, of course, the guy from Pakistan ended up having his desk right next to him. Not through any malice of management or facilities, but that just happens to be where the next available desk was. It didn't take long for the two of them sitting next to one another to realize that they had more in common than differences. Even though they never became friends, they worked together well, conversed, and got along very well. It was through living in another country not of their birth that allowed them the opportunity to see others for who they are versus what we are told to perceive.

As Americans, we have a reputation that precedes us everywhere we go. This is due to the policies of the US government and the people in the US who end up on the news. I am not going to use this book as an opportunity to voice an opinion on that reputation, but as travelers, we can use our encounters with others to show that we are not all like what people perceive us to be.

So if you are reading this while considering a move to Ireland or any other country, I would recommend you do it—not for money but for the opportunity to expand your world, to meet great people, and to live life to the fullest in the short span that we are on this planet. If you are reading this because you have already made the decision to move, congratulations! You have made the right choice.

Dedication and Thanks

I would like to thank the wonderful people I have met in my travels, especially in Ireland—all the way from the close friends I have made to the random drunk guy I met at the pub who interrupted my conversation to tell me that I should be proud of my Irish ancestry (I have none) and to stop using my fake sounding American accent. Personally, I'd say my American accent is pretty spot-on, having been born and raised in the Pacific Northwest. When traveling, the sites are what draw us to a destination, but it is the people we meet that make the journey memorable.

I would also like to dedicate this book to my grandmother. If there is a heaven, she is the only person I've ever met who truly deserves to be there. She is my "Supergram," the person who always encouraged my love of travel, and I wish she were still here to listen to my travel adventures.

Finally, if you enjoyed this book or found it useful, please recommend it to others as I could use the money. To read more about my travel experiences, check out www.milodenison.com.

18404113R00073

Made in the USA
San Bernardino, CA
13 January 2015